APPLICATION OF
BEHAVIOR ANALYSIS IN
LEISURE CONTEXTS
An Introductory Learning Manual

John Dattilo
Kari Kensinger

SAGAMORE
PUBLISHING

Publishers: Joseph J. Bannon and Peter L. Bannon
Sales and Marketing Managers: Emily Wakefield and Misti Gilles
Director of Development and Production: Susan M. Davis
Production Coordinator: Amy S. Dagit
Graphic Designer: Marissa Willison

Library of Congress Control Number: 2015948483
ISBN print edition: 978-1-57167-781-5
ISBN ebook: 978-1-57167-782-2

Printed in the United States.

SAGAMORE
PUBLISHING

1807 N. Federal Dr.
Urbana, IL 61801
www.sagamorepublishing.com

We dedicate this book to the many wonderful people
whose lives we have humbly attempted to enhance;
they have taught us much and touched our hearts.

Contents

Preface

This self-study learning manual is designed to introduce leisure service providers and students to behavior analysis and to assist them in developing and strengthening their skills in the application of associated techniques. The manual may be of value to other human service providers who are interested in applying behavior analysis techniques in situations designed to promote leisure engagement. It is our hope that this manual will assist those individuals who are dedicated to helping others engage in leisure. Leisure engagement leads to people experiencing meaning and enjoyment in their lives and, ultimately, increases their happiness and their ability to flourish.

This manual assumes that the reader has no previous knowledge of behavior analysis. The text contains five major sections with 21 associated chapters. The first section is devoted to examining and assessing behaviors that includes details on ways to describe, observe, and measure behaviors. This section also focuses on preference assessment and understanding behaviors through sequence analysis. The second section describes ways to influence behaviors by accelerating or decelerating behaviors. Procedures identified to accelerate behaviors conducive for leisure participation include positive reinforcement, token economies, and negative reinforcement. Extinction, punishment, and withdrawal of reinforcement are strategies designed to decelerate behaviors that are incompatible with leisure engagement. The third section identifies strategies to help teach behaviors facilitating leisure involvement that include schedules of reinforcement, shaping behaviors, chaining behaviors together, providing discrete trials, and developing functional communication. The fourth section of the manual provides details on promoting discrimination and generalization of behaviors with the purpose of encouraging maintenance and generalization of behaviors that facilitate leisure participation. The final section encourages readers to be consistent and informed in their application of behavior analysis procedures. As a result, this section contains information on supporting positive behaviors and using evidence-based practices.

Each chapter contains descriptions of procedures and associated exercises. A series of questions is provided at the end of each chapter to allow readers to test their acquisition and retention of the material addressed in the chapter. An answer key is included at the end of the manual to assist readers in evaluating their answers. We hope that readers find the manual to be helpful in improving their ability to interact with people in a helpful and respectful manner and create contexts that encourage leisure engagement.

1 INTRODUCTION TO BEHAVIOR ANALYSIS

Behavior analysis includes a systematic approach to understand behavior used by many professionals including those who provide leisure services. In recent years, the field of behavior analysis has grown in popularity because there is considerable research documenting the effectiveness of the approach. Although this book is about behavior analysis in leisure contexts, the concepts of leisure and play are embedded into the practice of behavior analysis.

An understanding of introductory techniques of behavior analysis can provide practitioners with helpful techniques to encourage positive behavior and discourage negative behaviors while people are engaged in leisure pursuits. The appropriate application of the procedures described in this book can encourage service providers to more effectively encourage individuals to engage in enjoyable and meaningful leisure experiences. An advantage of behavior analysis is that it can be used in any setting or circumstance where people interact with each other or their environment.

Behavior analysis is a systematic, performance-based, evaluative method for changing behavior. *Behavior* is any observable and measureable act, response, or movement by an individual. A behavior that is identified in need of improvement or change is referred to as a *target behavior*. Behavior analysis involves application of procedures designed to change behavior in a measurable manner.

Behavior analysis originates from the belief that **behaviors are learned**, rather than inherent, and can thus be changed by additional learning. Behavior analysis seeks to avoid inferences, vague reasoning, or undefined impulses as explanations for behavior. Whatever the behavior and whatever its cause, the behavior is present in an environment and is influenced and shaped by that environment. Behavior analysis focuses on the following:

- Observable and measureable behaviors
- The environment
- Goals and objectives
- Planning and implementation
- Teaching techniques
- Antecedent, behaviors, and consequences
- Evaluation and documentation

Behavior is the concern of behavior analysis, and it is behavior that can be changed. Behavior analysis is not a process concerned with attempts to determine the causes of behavior. The procedures used in behavior analysis focus on **observable and measurable behaviors** rather than presume influential internal agents. This approach does not deny the existence of internal agents, but rather concentrates specifically on the observable behaviors exhibited by an individual. Regardless of what is causing the behavior, it is behavior that can be observed and measured. Internal behavioral agents cannot be seen, nor can they be measured with any certainty or precision. Behavior is the focus of behavior analysis because it is behavior that can be changed by environmental manipulation.

Behavior analysis is based on the premise that humans are reactors to their environment. The **environment** contains all the circumstances, objects, people, behaviors, and conditions that an individual encounters. The emphasis in behavior analysis is placed on the relationship between changes in the environment and changes in the individual's behavior. Through environmental manipulation, an individual's behavior can change.

The procedures of behavior analysis are very compatible with the programming approach used by leisure service providers and other professionals. Based on the needs of participants, professionals develop **goals and objectives** designed to promote leisure engagement of program participants. The concentration on measurable behaviors in behavior analysis facilitates identification of participant needs and subsequent development of explicit objectives. These goals and objectives provide direction in determining the delivery of appropriate leisure programs.

Procedures used in behavior analysis are considered during the **planning** phase of developing leisure programs and applied during the actual **implementation** phase of the program. Professionals implementing behavior analysis techniques can assist participants in achieving program objectives by facilitating the acceleration of positive behaviors that are beneficial in a specific context, while decreasing behaviors that are disruptive of problematic for that context.

Application of the principles of behavior analysis can facilitate **identification of successful teaching techniques**. This identification encourages more frequent and systematic application of effective, precise, and clear learning strategies. As a result, behavior analysis techniques can be easily incorporated into professionals' existing repertoire of skills dedicated to facilitating the leisure experience and can be applied across a variety of settings.

Behavior analysis involves careful observation and analysis of individuals' behaviors by examining the relationship among behavioral **antecedents,** the **behaviors** themselves, and the **consequences** of these behaviors occurring in the environment. The emphasis in behavior analysis on the identification of observable and measurable target behaviors as well as on the antecedents and consequences of these behaviors enhances the ability of service providers to conduct systematic program evaluation.

Conducting effective program **evaluation** allows professionals to clearly document program effectiveness. **Documentation** of program effectiveness increases the ability of professionals to demonstrate the provision of quality services and subsequent enhancement of participants' leisure lifestyles.

Try the Following Exercise

Identify if the following statements are TRUE or FALSE by placing a T or an F in the space immediately to the left of the statement.

_____ 1. Implementation of principles associated with behavior analysis should be restricted to clinical settings.

_____ 2. A behavior is defined as any observable and measurable act, response, or movement by a person.

_____ 3. Behavior analysis originates from the belief that many behaviors occur spontaneously, without prior learning.

_____ 4. Behavior analysis focuses on measurable and observable behaviors rather than internal agents.

_____ 5. Behavior analysis is primarily concerned with the relationship of an individual's behavior and associated feelings.

_____ 6. The environment contains all the circumstances, objects, people, behaviors, and conditions that a person encounters.

_____ 7. The professional develops goals and objectives based on the interests and expertise of existing personnel.

_____ 8. Procedures used in behavior analysis should be considered during the planning, implementation, and evaluation phases of a leisure program.

_____ 9. Behavior analysis focuses on the individuals' behavior and is not concerned with what occurs before or after the target behavior.

_____ 10. Effective program evaluation increases the ability of professionals to document program effectiveness.

Please see the next page to determine the accuracy of your responses.

All statements associated with odd numbers are FALSE and all statements corresponding to even numbers are TRUE.

In review, the following are **characteristics of behavior analysis**:

- Evaluates methods for changing **behaviors**
- Originates from the belief the behaviors are **learned**
- Focuses on **observable and measurable** behaviors
- Based on premise that humans are reactors to the **environment**
- Is compatible with recreation **programming**
- Should be considered during program **planning** and **implementation**
- Focuses on **antecendents, behaviors**, and **consequences**
- Facilitates **evaluation** of behavior and programs

You have now completed the introductory material on behavior analysis. Next you can evaluate how well you retained the information on the following pages.

Test Your Knowledge of an Introduction to Behavior Analysis

1. Behavior may be defined as:

    a. a systematic method for changing the environment.
    b. observable and measurable acts, responses, or movements by an individual.
    c. the emotional response of individuals to unfamiliar environments.
    d. the physical movements or actions of an individual.
    e. the presence of internal impulses that cause an individual to act in an inappropriate manner.

2. Behavior analysis is a systematic method for:

    a. altering or changing behavior.
    b. determining the causes of behavior.
    c. determining the presence of internal agents.
    d. estimating the effects of behavior in social environments.

3. Behavior analysis procedures may be used:

    a. in any setting where humans interact with each other or their environment.
    b. only by certified therapeutic recreation specialists.
    c. only in clinical settings.
    d. only with individuals who have emotional limitations.
    e. only with individuals who have physical disabilities.

4. Behavior analysis is based on the premise that:

    a. behaviors are determined by internal agents.
    b. behaviors are inherent, rather than learned.
    c. behaviors are learned, rather than inherent.
    d. internal agents are determined by behaviors.
    e. internal agents are determined by environments.

5. A target behavior that is:

    a. a model to be adopted by an individual in a behavior analysis program.
    b. aimed at modifying the environment.
    c. exhibited by the individual who is applying behavior analysis techniques.
    d. the focus of systematic efforts aimed at altering it.
    e. to remain unchanged by an individual in a behavior analysis program.

6. Behavior analysis focuses on:

    a. hypotheses to be tested.
    b. individuals with disabilities.
    c. inferences.
    d. internal agents.
    e. observable and measureable behaviors.

7. A basis for behavior analysis is the belief that:

   a. change in internal agents can cause change in the environment.
   b. changes in the environment can effect a change in behavior.
   c. internal agents can be measured with the same precision as external agents.
   d. the cause of a behavior must be identified before the behavior can be modified.
   e. it is easier to identify internal agents than it is external agents.

8. Behavior analysis emphasized the concept that:

   a. behavior cannot be influenced by environmental manipulation.
   b. humans are not influenced by their environments.
   c. humans react only to internal agents.
   d. humans react to their environment.
   e. target behaviors must remain unchanged.

9. Behavior analysis is based on:

   a. environmental manipulation.
   b. manipulation of internal agents.
   c. the belief that behavior is an inherent trait.
   d. the belief that clinical settings are the best environments for behavior analysis procedures to be applied.
   e. the belief that target behaviors must not be changed.

10. Environmental manipulation can facilitate:

    a. change in an individual's behavior.
    b. the determination of causes of behavior.
    c. the measurement of internal agents.
    d. the reduction of the influence of leisure as a determinant of lifestyle.
    e. the reduction of the strength of internal agents.

11. Behavior analysis procedures are:

    a. compatible with the concept that behavior is inherent.
    b. compatible with programming approaches used by leisure service providers.
    c. incompatible with programming approaches used by leisure service providers.
    d. most useful when applied in clinical settings.
    e. most useful when focused on internal agents.

12. Behavior analysis procedures should first be considered during the:

    a. acceleration phase of leisure programs.
    b. delivery phase of leisure programs.
    c. evaluation phase of leisure programs.
    d. implementation phase of leisure programs.
    e. planning phase of leisure programs.

13. Behavior analysis procedures should:

    a. decrease the strength of behaviors that are appropriate in a specific context.
    b. increase the strength of behaviors that are appropriate in a specific context.
    c. increase the strength of behaviors that are inappropriate in a specific context.
    d. increase the strength of internal agents.
    e. neutralize the effects of environmental manipulation.

14. Behavior analysis techniques are:

    a. easily incorporated into the repertoire of skills possessed by recreation professionals.
    b. too sophisticated to be applied by recreation professionals.
    c. useful only in clinical settings.
    d. useful only in natural environments.
    e. useful only when applied to individuals with disabilities.

15. Behavior analysis involves the analysis of behavior and their:

    a. antecedents and consequences.
    b. effect on the environment.
    c. effect on recreation professionals.
    d. expression during leisure
    e. internal causes.

Now that you have completed the evaluation, please check your answers with the ones in the back of the book. If needed, review the introductory material on behavior analysis and try the evaluation again. When you are satisfied with your acquisition of the information and understand the concepts, begin work on the next chapter.

2 DESCRIBE BEHAVIORS

The initial step in changing a behavior requires accurate observation and description of the behavior. An accurate description of behavior is dependent on the use of terms that specify observable and measurable actions. Picture in your mind a group of children who are hyperactive. What were the children doing? Were they running around in circles, bouncing up and down, rocking back and forth, or perhaps talking rapidly and gasping for breath? The term "hyperactive" could be applied to any of these actions. However, it would not clearly describe the precise actions or behaviors in which the children were engaging. In this case, "hyperactive" is a label, an interpretation of a group's behavior. In this text, when asked to discuss a behavior, the reader is discouraged from using labels and encouraged to use terms that describe the observable and measurable behavior that is occurring.

Terms that describe behavior must specify actions that are:

- **observable**
- **measurable**

Behaviors that are observable and measurable are called **overt behaviors**. *Overt behaviors* can be identified with the five senses and, when described, generally mean the same thing to different people. **Covert behaviors** are not as readily identifiable as overt behaviors. Terms that are applied to indicate covert behaviors are not as specific and may not mean the same thing to different people. *Covert terms* are most often used to describe the interpretations made by an observer about another individual's behavior or attitude and, therefore, may be subject to many different interpretations.

When describing behaviors, we are often required to write **behaviorally specific statements.** *A behaviorally specific statement* is one that depicts explicit actions (overt behaviors). It does not include what we might assume the person being observed thinks or feels. It does not refer to covert behaviors, which are subject to many different interpretations. A behaviorally specific statement deals only with actions that are observable and measurable.

The following are guidelines for describing behaviors:

- **Use overt terms that describe observable and measurable behaviors.**
- **Use behaviorally specific statements to depict explicit actions.**

Listed on the following page is a series of terms. In the space provided to the left of the numbers that precede the terms, place a "C" for those that describe covert behaviors and an "O" for those that describe overt behaviors.

_O_   1. laughs

_O_   2. talks

_C_   3. lazy

_O_   4. runs

_C_   5. polite

_C_   6. depressed

_C_   7. selfish

_O_   8. smiles

_O_   9. screams

_C_   10. industrious

_O_   11. cries

_C_   12. upset

_C_   13. indifferent

_C_   14. obstinate

_C_   15. angry

_C_   16. anxious

_C_   17. sad

_O_   18. kicks

_O_   19. throws

_C_   20. apathetic

If you placed a "C" in front of 3, 5–7, 10, 12–17, and 20, you are on the right track! All of these words are subjective interpretations of behaviors or feelings. These terms do not describe directly observable or measurable behaviors; they are covert terms. Because the remaining words are descriptive of specific, concrete actions, they apply to behaviors that are observable and measurable. They are overt terms and should have an "O" placed in front of them.

Now, in the space provided to the immediate right of the covert terms, record overt actions that may describe the vague covert behaviors. If you have difficulty thinking of observable behaviors, review this section.

Once you have completed the exercise, please turn to the next page and evaluate your understanding of the material presented on describing behaviors.

Test Your Knowledge of Describing Behaviors

1. For a behavior to be considered overt, it must have which of the following characteristics?

   a. approachable, observable
   b. approachable, countable
   c. believable, controllable
   d. believable, measurable
   e. observable, measurable

2. What do covert terms describe?

   a. behavioral antecedents
   b. labels and feelings
   c. overt behaviors
   d. precise actions
   e. target behaviors

3. Which of the following is written in behaviorally specific terms?

   a. Betty is angry with Rondrea.
   b. Camilo stated "I like you" to William.
   c. Elijah does not like Marco.
   d. Colin enjoys being with Diane.
   e. Mahalia gets upset when she sees Cathy.

4. A label may be described as:

   a. a precise description of an individual's behavior.
   b. a term that depicts a group of specific actions.
   c. an observer's interpretation of an individual's behavior.
   d. essential for depicting overt behavior.
   e. necessary for conveying accurate meaning.

5. Terms used to indicate covert behaviors:

   a. accurately describe the observed individual's feelings.
   b. exclude subjective interpretation.
   c. depict precise actions.
   d. generally mean the same thing to different people.
   e. may not mean the same thing to different people.

6. What is the term used to describe behaviors that are observable and measurable?

   a. antecedents
   b. consequences
   c. covert
   d. feelings
   e. overt

7. Your assistant has described Demetri as being an angry person. Which measurable behaviors might your assistant have observed Demetri exhibiting?

   a. anxious, hit others, upset
   b. anxious, irritable, unreasonable
   c. hit others, kicked, spit
   d. hot headed, upset, psychotic
   e. illogical, ridiculous, unsatisfied

8. An observer watching the leisure education session said Tyrone was a nice boy with a good attitude. Which measurable behavior might the observer be attempting to describe?

   a. attentive
   b. delighted
   c. interested
   d. smiling
   e. studious

9. Which of the following is a behaviorally specific statement?

   a. Jabari is dumb.
   b. José is acting silly.
   c. Julian is a show-off.
   d. Judy is smart.
   e. Jacinta is walking.

10. Five observers were asked to write a statement describing overt behavior on the part of any participant in the recreation center's exercise program. Which of the following is a behaviorally specific statement?

    a. Amy was depressed today.
    b. Chan is a leader.
    c. Denise is extremely intelligent.
    d. Mary threw a ball through the window.
    e. Sabina got angry while playing basketball.

11. Which of the following is a behaviorally specific statement?

    a. Angie argues most of the time.
    b. Ghania attended the baseball game.
    c. Thiago is very active in sports.
    d. Teresa is an outspoken person.
    e. Thomas enjoys playing tennis.

12. Which statement is written in behaviorally specific terms?

    a. Alex was so upset he ran out of the room.
    b. Sofia answered the questions correctly.
    c. Carol slammed the door in anger.
    d. Josip enjoys reading stories every day.
    e. Leon became depressed over the loss of his kids.

13. Which pair of statements is written in behaviorally specific terms?

    a. Ivan is in a world of his own on Saturdays.
       Nathan cried three times because he was upset.
    b. Juan was frustrated after losing two games.
       Ivan is in a world of his own on Saturdays.
    c. Gaetano cried three times because he was upset.
       Patricia asked a question in ceramics class.
    d. Catalina asked a question in ceramics class.
       Shirley yelled after she was hit by the ball.
    e. Shan yelled after she was hit by the ball.
       Kadeem was frustrated after losing two games.

14. Which of the following is a sequence of overt behaviors?

    a. active, jumps, excited
    b. angry, upset, cries
    c. frustrated, depressed, anxious
    d. lazy, sleeping, tired
    e. smiles, laughs, talks

15. A participant described Obasi as being "unsociable." Which observable behavior may have led the participant to that conclusion?

    a. easily distracted
    b. extremely confused
    c. does not talk
    d. often moody
    e. very inhibited

Now that you have completed the evaluation, please check your answers with the ones in the back of the book. If needed, review the material on describing behaviors and try the evaluation again. When you are satisfied with your acquisition of the information and understand your errors, turn the page and begin work on the next chapter.

3 OBSERVE BEHAVIORS

Accurate observation of behavior is essential for the application of behavior analysis. Effective observation is necessary to assess the quantity and extent of the behavior exhibited by the program participants. Observation cannot begin until the target behaviors are clearly described.

When the target behaviors have been accurately described, observation may proceed. This requires a clear determination of the method of observation to be used. Although there are many acceptable ways to observe and record behavior, the four most common methods will be considered at this time. These four recording methods are the following:

- **frequency (tally)**
- **duration**
- **interval**
- **instantaneous time sampling**

Frequency recording involves counting and recording each occurrence of a behavior within a given time frame. It is primarily used when the identified behavior occurs **at a low rate** and **lasts for brief periods of time**. Frequency recording is a particularly appropriate method of observing behavior when the target behavior has an **easily defined beginning and ending.** Behaviors of this nature are termed *discrete* and they involve no uncertainty as to when they begin and end. This makes frequency recording an easily accomplished task for the observer. When a goal is to increase or decrease the number of times a behavior occurs, frequency recording is the appropriate method of observation.

Frequency (Tally) Recording Method (123456)

For instance, a child in a preschool play program may frequently engage in the inappropriate behavior of throwing the toys against a wall. Throwing a toy against a wall is a discrete behavior that is readily observed. If the first step in modifying the behavior is to assess how often it occurs, frequency recording would be an appropriate observation method to employ. The child could be observed during a specified time period for as many days or sessions deemed necessary. Observation would simply require tallying the number of times the child threw a toy against a wall during the specified time period.

Further analysis can occur when using the frequency count. The observer can note the number of occurrences of a particular behavior during a specified amount of time and determine the rate of the behavior. For instance, a coach may count the number of times a basketball player makes a lay-up in one minute. Another option, using the frequency method, is to calculate the percentage or accuracy of an individual's performance. Percentage involves dividing the number of times the behavior occurs by the number of trials available to the individual. A person playing a card game may correctly follow directions eight out of ten times, resulting in a score of 80%.

Guidelines for the application of frequency recording are as follows:

1. Use with behaviors that occur at a **low rate** and last for a **brief duration**.
2. Use when behaviors are **discrete**.
3. Use when the goal is to increase or decrease the **number of times** the behavior occurs.

Duration Recording Method

A second method that is commonly used in observing behaviors is duration recording. *Duration recording* involves recording the length of time the target behavior occurs during an observation period. When using duration recording, the key consideration is **how long the behavior lasts,** rather than the number of times the behavior occurred.

Duration recording is employed when the behavior occurs at a **low frequency** and lasts for an **extended time period.** The observer needs only to have a stopwatch or some other timing device to accurately record the duration of a behavior. However, duration recording does require that the behavior under observation have **definite starting and ending points.** As a reminder, when a behavior has a clear starting and ending point it is identified as a *discrete behavior*.

When a goal is to increase or decrease the length of time a behavior occurs, duration recording is the appropriate method of observation. It may also be used when a goal is to reduce or eliminate a behavior.

Duration Recording Method

By way of illustration, a leisure service professional may be interested in increasing the amount of time a participant spends in cooperative play with other particiants. Before initiating efforts aimed at increasing cooperative activities, it is necessary to have some knowledge of how much time is currently expended by the participant in the activity. During the observation periods, the leisure service professional would need only to use a timing device to measure and record the length of time the child engaged in cooperative play with others. Intervention strategies to increase the length of time could then be determined and implemented.

Guidelines for the application of duration recording are as follows:

1. Use when behavior occurs at a **low frequency** and lasts for an **extended time** period.
2. Use when behavior is **discrete.**
3. Use this procedure when the goal is to increase or decrease the **length of time** of the occurrence.

Interval Recording Method

Interval recording is the third common method of behavior observation. *Interval recording* requires that a **block of time be divided into short segments of equal length.** The intervals should be short enough to allow the recording of separate occurrences of behavior but long enough to facilitate accurate observation.

> For instance, a 30-minute block of time could be divided into intervals of 15 seconds each. The participant is observed during each of the intervals and the target behavior recorded if it occurs at any time during an interval.

It makes no difference if the behavior occurs once or several times during an interval; it simply is recorded as having occurred. If the behavior lasts over several intervals, it is recorded in each of the intervals that it occurs.

Interval Recording Method

> As an example, a leisure service professional is engaged in teaching a small group of youths to play some simple table games at a recreation center. One of the youth, Lisa, may be disruptive by frequently kicking a table leg. An observer elects to divide a 30-minute period of the table game session into intervals of 15 seconds each. If the kicking behavior occurs once during a 15-second interval, the observer records the incident by making a tally for that interval. If Lisa kicks the table leg several times during a 15-second interval, the observer still makes only one tally for that interval. If Lisa kicks the table leg for 45 consecutive seconds, the observer still simply records a single tally for each of the intervals during which the kicking occurred.

Guidelines for the application of interval recording are as follows:

1. Segment observation period into short intervals.
2. Observe during the predetermined intervals.
3. Record if the target behavior occurred during an interval.

Instantaneous Time Sampling Recording Method

Instantaneous time sampling is another common method of behavior observation. With *instantaneous time sampling*, behaviors are also recorded as occurring or not occurring during intervals when the participant is being observed. However, the time period does not have to be divided into shorter segments of equal length and the observer only examines the behavior at the end of the interval. The observation intervals must be of **equal length** but they **can be separated by larger blocks of time**. This technique of behavior observation is appropriate when the target behavior occurs at a **high frequency** and the observer **does not have the time to continuously observe** participants.

Instantaneous Time Sampling Recording Method

To illustrate, while playing video games a participant is noticed as frequently rocking his body back and forth. A staff member is asked to observe the frequency of this behavior but does not have the time to devote to uninterrupted observation because she must also attend to other duties. The staff member may decide to observe the resident for a five-second interval at the end of every 10-minute period. A tally for the rocking behavior is made if it is observed during the five-second observation interval. This strategy allows the staff member to attend to her other duties and still make recordings of the target behavior.

Guidelines for using instantaneous time sampling recording are as follows:

1. Segment observation period into intervals.
2. Observe at the end of an interval and record if the target behavior occurred during the momentary observation.

On the next page is a list of behaviors with corresponding frequency, duration, and observation information. Write the most appropriate observation method for each behavior on the line provided.

1. Arturo hits his head with his hand at a frequency of 934 per day; each hit lasts about one second. He may hit his head rapidly several times in succession and then refrain for several minutes. It is difficult to determine precisely when the behavior starts or stops.

   _____

2. Cindy fails to attend the swimming program. The leisure service professional would like to submit a report to her social worker about her absences.

   _____

3. Lev puts toys in her mouth on an average of once per hour. Each time this inappropriate behavior occurs, it lasts for five seconds.

   _____

4. Louis engages in conversation two times for approximately five minutes within an hour-discussion period. Because of the nature of the program, it is difficult for the recreation leader to constantly observe Louis' behavior.

   _____

5. Katrina practices walking three times per day and walks an average of seven minutes.

   _____

6. Sarah remains at the sculpting table on an average of twice per class for about four minutes each time she is at the table. The leisure service professional is unable to continuously observe at her station.

   _____

7. During a free play period, Matthew screams loudly three times. Each outburst lasts approximately 14 minutes.

   _____

8. While playing basketball, Sophia uses offensive language often (100 times) during a game.

   _____

Please see the next page for suggested answers and a description of the rationale for the selections.

Frequency recording should be used for situations 2 and 3. Each of these behaviors occurs at a relatively low frequency and each has readily identifiable starting and ending points. In addition, the behavior described in situation 3 is of a short duration and the behavior described in situation 2 simply occurs or does not occur. These factors combine to make frequency recording the most appropriate observation method to use in both instances. The goal would be to increase the number of times Cindy attends the swimming program and to decrease the number of times Lev puts toys in her mouth.

Duration recording should be used for situations 5 and 7. Each of these behaviors occurs at a low frequency and lasts a considerable length of time. Both behaviors also have definite starting and ending points, thus lending themselves to duration recording with a minimum of difficulty. The goal of a behavior modification program would be to increase the length of time Katrina spends in walking and to decrease the amount of time Matthew spends in screaming.

Interval recording would be the appropriate observation method to use in situations 1 and 8. Both behaviors occur at a high rate of frequency and both can be recorded as having occurred or not occurred during specified time intervals. The behavior described in situation 1 might be difficult to observe for an entire day but would be easily observed for a single block of time, such as a 30- or 60-minute period divided into a series of short, equal segments. The behavior described in situation 8 would be more easily observed and recorded by intervals. The goal of a behavior modification program in each of these situations would be to reduce the number of times the inappropriate behavior occurred.

Instantaneous time sampling should be used in situations 4 and 6. The decision to use instantaneous time sampling is based primarily on the availability (or the lack thereof) of the observer. In circumstances such as those described in these two situations, the observer would have little latitude in choosing a method of observation. Instantaneous time sampling would allow the observer to attend to other duties and still make some observation of behaviors. The goal of a behavior modification program would probably be to increase the amount of time Louis engages in conversation and Sarah spends at the sculpting table.

When you have completed this exercise, please go to the next page and evaluate the degree to which you understand the information on methods of observing behaviors.

Test Your Knowledge of Observing Behaviors

1. You are interested in determining how long Darlene engages in toy play. Which type of observation schedule will be used?

   a. duration
   b. frequency
   c. interval
   d. percentage
   e. time sampling

2. Momar uses an excessive amount of inappropriate verbalizations (average: 10 per minute) during leisure education class. Because of the high number of inappropriate verbalizations, what is the best observation schedule to use?

   a. duration
   b. frequency
   c. interval
   d. ratio
   e. time sampling

3. Which of the following would be best observed during a frequency count?

   a. biting (frequency: 10/week, duration: 1 second)
   b. grabbing (frequency: 4/day, duration: 2 minutes)
   c. rocking (frequency: 20/minute, duration: 2 seconds)
   d. screaming (frequency: 1/month, duration: 3 hours)
   e. spitting (frequency: 90/day, duration: 1 second)

4. Donna rarely engages in social interaction with other participants in the crafts program (average: once per one hour session). You are interested in the number of times she initiates interaction. Because of the low number of interactions she engages in, what observation schedule should you decide to use?

   a. duration
   b. frequency
   c. interval
   d. percentage
   e. time sampling

5. When wanting to increase or decrease the time a behavior lasts, which measurement method is best to use?

   a. duration recording
   b. frequency recording
   c. interval recording
   d. ratio recording
   e. time sampling recording

6. When is it best to use a frequency count?

    a. high frequency and high duration
    b. low frequency and high duration
    c. low frequency and low duration
    d. medium frequency and low duration
    e. low frequency and medium duration

7. While participating in tumbling, Julia often sits on the floor, screams, cries, and hits her knees with her hands for long periods of time. First, your objective is to decrease the time of the incident, therefore you would observe the behavior in relation to which of the following?

    a. duration
    b. frequency
    c. interval
    d. occurrence
    e. ratio

8. Which behavior would best be observed using instantaneous time sampling?

    a. biting (frequency: 3/week, duration: 1 second)
    b. grabbing (frequency: 4/day, duration: 2 minutes)
    c. hitting (frequency: 10/day, duration: 2 seconds)
    d. screaming (frequency: 1/month, duration: 3 hours)
    e. spitting (frequency: 90/day, duration: 1 second)

9. When Steven arrives at the soccer field, he often climbs a tree and sits on a limb for long periods of time. Initially, you want to decrease the time of the incident, therefore you would observe the behavior in relationship to its:

    a. duration.
    b. frequency.
    c. interval.
    d. occurrence.
    e. ratio.

10. Tao initiates conversation at a low rate and low duration while playing on the playground. You would like to increase the number of times the behavior occurs. Which observation method would be best to use?

    a. duration
    b. frequency
    c. interval
    d. ratio
    e. sampling

11. Discrete behaviors are behaviors that:

    a. are deemed to be socially acceptable.
    b. are difficult to measure because they do not have definite beginning and ending points.
    c. have been identified as being in need of modification.
    d. have definite beginning and ending points.
    e. may only be observed by use of instantaneous time sampling.

12. Accurate observation of behavior must be preceded by:

    a. measures that will insure the anonymity of the observer.
    b. precise identification of a target behavior.
    c. pre-determination of an intervention strategy.
    d. procedures that will prevent the program participant from knowing that he/she is being observed.
    e. selection of an observation method.

13. Which of the following is not an appropriate guideline for the application of frequency recording?

    a. Use when the goal is to increase the number of times the behavior occurs.
    b. Use when the behavior lasts for an extended period of time.
    c. Use when the behavior lasts for a short period of time.
    d. Use with behaviors that are discrete.
    e. Use with behaviors that occur at a low rate.

14. Which of the following is not an appropriate guideline for the application of duration recording?

    a. Use when the behavior is discrete.
    b. Use when the behavior lasts for an extended period of time.
    c. Use when the behavior occurs at a low frequency.
    d. Use when the goal is to increase the length of time the behavior occurs.
    e. Use when the goal is to increase the number of times the behavior occurs.

15. Instantaneous time sampling recording is appropriate for use when the:

    a. observation period cannot be divided into intervals.
    b. observer does not have the time to continuously observe the program participant.
    c. target behavior lasts for a short period of time.
    d. target behavior occurs at a low frequency.
    e. use of a time device is not required.

After completing the evaluation on observing behaviors, please check your answers with the ones listed in the back of the book. If you did not perform as well as you would like, try reviewing the material in this section and give the evaluation another try. When you are satisfied with your retention of the information, please turn the page and begin work on the next chapter.

4 MEASURE BEHAVIORS

When target behaviors are being described, observed, and recorded, a considerable amount of data are generated. To be useful these data must be displayed in an efficient and clearly understood manner. The picture obtained from this display may be developed by means of a graph.

A *graph* is a diagram that depicts the interrelationship between the program or treatment and the behaviors of the participants. The major advantage of a graph is its ability to quickly convey the status of a target behavior or the effectiveness of intervention or treatment strategies. It can provide a clear understanding of the past status of target behaviors. The graph also has potential for use as a predictor for target behavior change. A graph may be the most readily used tool available for representation of the data systematically gathered in a leisure program.

A graph involves a vertical line and a horizontal line that are connected to form an "L-shaped" figure. The vertical line may be referred to as the ***ordinate axis***; the horizontal line is referred to as the ***abscissa axis***. The ordinate of a graph depicts the behavior or the method of measurement used to observe the behavior. The abscissa represents the length or periods of time during which the behavior was observed. The ordinate and abscissa of a graph are subdivided into uniform units of measurement and time, respectively.

The common methods of behavior measurement represented on the ordinate of a graph include the following:

- Frequency
- Duration
- Percentage
- Rate

Each of these measurements is appropriate for use in specific situations. When desiring to illustrate how often a particular behavior occurs during a given period of time, the ordinate would be labeled to depict **frequency**.

> For example, if a leisure service professional wished to depict how often Vada voluntarily participated in discussions during daily leisure education sessions over a specified period of time, a graph might be labeled as follows:

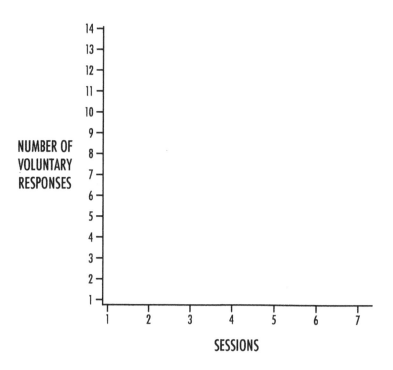

When the intent is to show how long a behavior lasts during specified time periods, the ordinate would be labeled to depict **duration**.

For example, if a leisure service professional wished to show the length of time Jafar remained seated during 30-minute story-telling sessions, a graph might be labeled as follows:

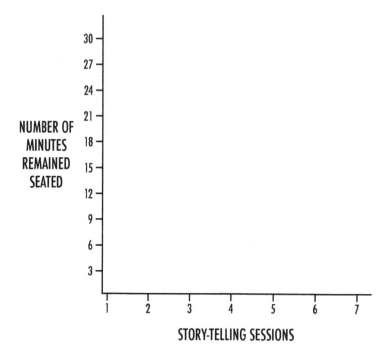

A graph may also be used to depict the percentages of time particular behaviors occur or any other factors that lend themselves to expression by **percentages**.

For example, Logan, who attends a day camp program, requires the use of the restroom facilities several times during the morning sessions but often refuses to wash his hands after toileting. A graph that illustrates the percentage of time he engaged in the desired behavior of hand washing could be labeled as follows:

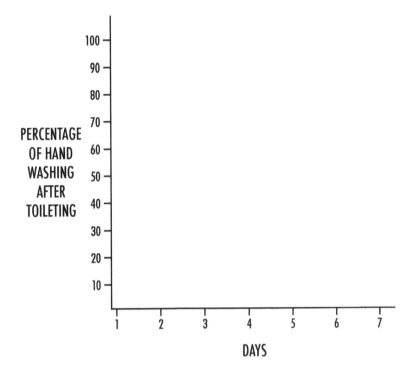

In addition, a graph may be used to illustrate the **rate** of a particular behavior. In so doing, the ordinate of a graph would contain units representing the number of responses divided by the length of time required to elicit those responses.

For example, Eden, a woman attending sports class, may be given several one-minute trials to see how many basketball lay-ups she can make. A graph that depicts her rate of success for this particular basketball shot could be labeled as follows:

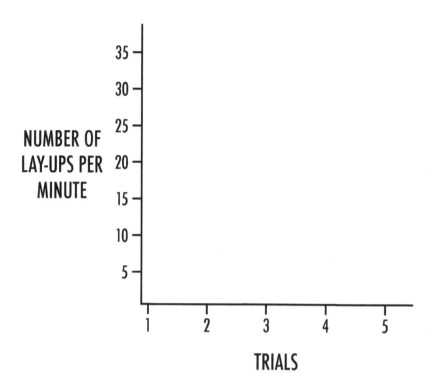

The common measurements represented on the ordinate of a graph include the following:

- Frequency
- Duration
- Percentage
- Rate

The abscissa of a graph always represents the units of time used to observe and measure the behavior represented on the ordinate. The abscissa includes such units of time as minutes, hours, days, weeks, or months. It could also include units representing time periods such as classes, sessions, trials, and so forth. Follow these directions to successfully graph the occurrences of a behavior:

- After the unit of time (on the abscissa) has passed, go up the **ordinate** until you come to the number corresponding to the behavior's occurrence.
- Move directly across to the right of that number until you come to the place above the number on the **abscissa** that corresponds with the time the observation was made, and make a dot.
- **Plot** the graph by starting with the dot that represents the first observation.
- **Draw a straight line** between it and the dot that represents the second observation.
- **Connect the second dot to the third dot** and proceed in this fashion until all the dots are connected.

On the graph located below, graph the following data, following the previous instructions.

- Day 1. Frequency 24
- Day 2. Frequency 26
- Day 3. Frequency 16
- Day 4. Frequency 12
- Day 5. Frequency 18
- Day 6. Frequency 10
- Day 7. Frequency 4
- Day 8. Frequency 6
- Day 9. Frequency 2
- Day 10. Frequency 0

When you have completed graphing the 10 days, please turn to the next page. If your graph looks like the one on the following page, you have the right idea!

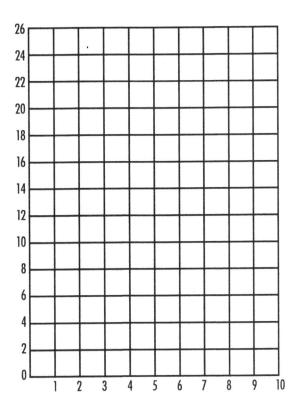

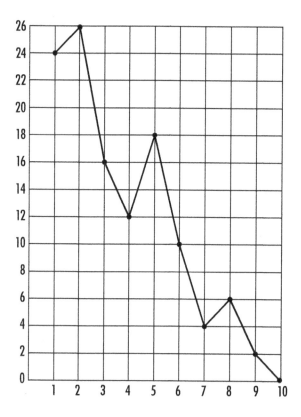

Prior to starting a program, an observation period occurs. This observation period is termed a ***baseline***. During a baseline, no attempt is made to change or influence the behavior, except perhaps to set the occasion for the behavior to occur. The length of time taken for the baseline varies according to the severity of the behavior.

Baseline observation on a graph is set aside from the remainder of the graph by a vertical dotted line drawn between the last baseline observation and the first treatment observation. The baseline period is the pretreatment record, which allows comparison with data from the intervention phases later in the program.

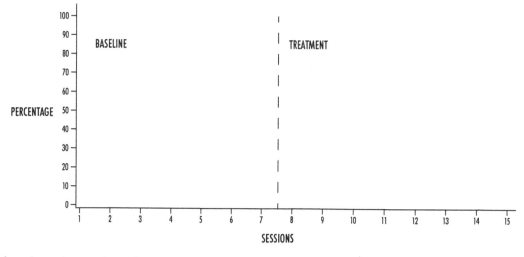

Once data have been plotted on the graph, there are three different interpretations that can be made from the information.

1. If the general slope of the line is upward, the behavior is increasing. This movement is termed acceleration.

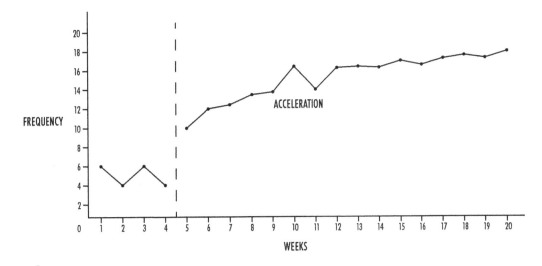

2. If the general slope of the line is downward, the behavior is decreasing. This movement is termed deceleration.

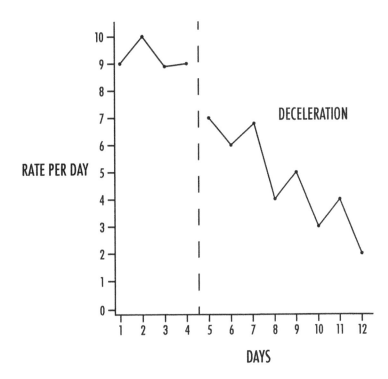

3. If the slope of the line is parallel with the horizontal line, the behavior is neither increasing nor decreasing. The behavior is said to be **maintained**.

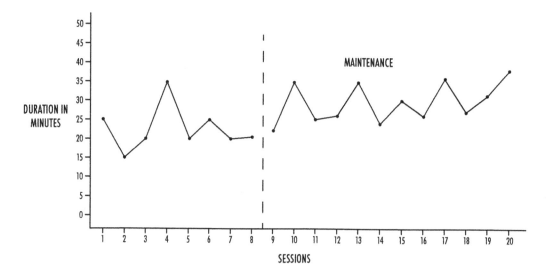

Three possible interpretations of data plotted on a graph:

1. Acceleration

2. Deceleration

3. Maintenance

You have now completed the information on graphing. Please go to the next page and evaluate how well you retained the material.

Test Your Knowledge of Measuring Behaviors

1. When measuring the duration of a behavior, what units are represented on the ordinate of a graph?

    a. how often the behavior occurs
    b. the accuracy of performance
    c. the extent to which the behavior returns
    d. the length of time a behavior occurs
    e. the number of responses divided by the time required

2. Prior to the initiation of an intervention strategy, Jia was observed for a week. Her daily rate of crying was 27 during this time period. Intervention began at the start of the second week and her daily rate dropped to 10. During the third week, it reached a daily rate of 38. A revision in the strategy was made during the fourth week and the daily rate dropped to 20. What was Jia's average daily rate of crying during baseline?

    a. 38
    b. 27
    c. 20
    d. 10
    e. 0

3. When measuring the rate of behavior, what units are represented on the ordinate of a graph?

    a. how often the behavior occurs
    b. the accuracy of the performance
    c. the extent to which the behavior returns
    d. the length of time a behavior occurs
    e. the number of responses divided by the time required

4. What is the term used to describe the observation period prior to the initiation of an intervention strategy?

    a. baseline
    b. deprivation
    c. duration
    d. acceleration
    e. maintenance

5. When measuring the frequency of the behavior, what units are represented on the ordinate of a graph?

    a. how often the behavior occurs
    b. the accuracy of performance
    c. the extent to which the behavior returns
    d. the length of time the behavior occurs
    e. the number of responses divided by the time required

6. What does the abscissa represent on a graph?

    a. numbers
    b. percentage
    c. rate
    d. space
    e. time

7. When measuring the percentage of the behavior, what units are represented on the ordinate of a graph?

    a. how often the behavior returns
    b. the accuracy of the performance
    c. the extent to which the behavior returned
    d. the length of time a behavior occurs
    e. the number of responses divided by the time required

8. What are the possible units of measurement included on the ordinate?

    a. minutes, days, weeks, months
    b. duration, percentage, rate, frequency
    c. frequency, interval, ratio, percentage
    d. rate, duration, minutes, weeks
    e. ratio, interval, time sampling, rate

9. What is the term used to describe the behavior that is pictured by the slope of the line pointing downward on a graph?

    a. accelerating
    b. being maintained
    c. decelerating
    d. negatively reinforced
    e. positively reinforced

10. When the slope of the line on a graph is pointing upward, the behavior is:

    a. accelerating.
    b. being extinguished.
    c. being maintained.
    d. being punished.
    e. decelerating.

11. A graph is a diagram that depicts the relationship between:

    a. rate and duration.
    b. the observer and the program participant.
    c. the ordinate and the rate of behavior.
    d. the target behavior and the terminal behavior.
    e. two variables.

12. A major advantage of a graph is its ability to:

    a. describe the target behavior.
    b. predict baseline data.
    c. quickly indicate the relationship between the observer and the program participant.
    d. quickly indicate the status of the target behavior.
    e. select an intervention strategy.

13. On a graph, baseline data and treatment data are separated by:

    a. a two-week time period.
    b. a horizontal dotted line.
    c. a vertical dotted line.
    d. a vertical solid line.
    e. the ordinate.

14. The length of time required for gathering baseline data depends on the:

    a. complexity of the treatment strategy.
    b. cooperation of the observed.
    c. length of the treatment time.
    d. severity of the target behavior.
    e. skill of the observer.

15. When the line on a graph is generally parallel to the abscissa, the behavior is:
    a. accelerating.
    b. being extinguished.
    c. being maintained.
    d. being punished.
    e. decelerating.

Now that you have completed the evaluation, please check your answers with the ones listed in the back of the book. When you are satisfied with your retention of the information, you are ready to begin work on the next chapter.

5 | ASSESS PREFERENCES

In previous chapters, the topic of behavioral analysis is identified as being directly connected to the leisure programming process. The first step of that process typically involves assessment, which might include working with a person to conduct a needs assessment, a functional skills assessment, or a preference assessment. A preference assessment is a means to rank activities or items based on their desirability.

Since leisure engagement involves participation in a preferred activity, the intent of a preference assessment is to distinguish between those activities or items that are highly preferred and those that are less preferred. While professionals often use preference assessments to determine participant **leisure interests,** this approach can also be used to identify potential types of **reinforcement,** such as desirable activities and preferred community locations.

The most common way to determine if someone would like to engage in an activity is to ask the person. However, there are various people who experience challenges with expressing their preferences. Some individuals may have speech or hearing deficits that make it difficult for them to express their preferences. Other people encounter difficulty with expressive speech due to cognitive problems such as aphasia (a neural disruption in the comprehension and expression of communication) or having sustained a traumatic brain injury. Challenges associated with expressing preferences can also be a result of mental health problems such as depression or bipolar disorder (a mental disorder involving periods of elevated mood and times of depression). Also, some people who are shy and quiet may relinquish their opportunity to express their preferences to other people who are a bit more loquacious. Other people may have recently immigrated to the country and therefore experience challenges related to their expressive and receptive language.

In addition to various conditions and situations that may create challenges for people to communicate their preferences and interests, there are some people who feel pressured in the presence of an authority figure, such as a leisure service professional, and, therefore, will acquiesce. *Acquiescence* involves an individual acting or verbally answering in a particular way that indicates agreement with another person or is a response that is thought to be how the other person would like the individual to respond. Often this other person is deemed to be in a position of authority.

Given these challenges in determining preferences, the following six types of preference assessments commonly used in behavior analysis are presented in this chapter.

- Personal nomination
- Single stimulus
- Paired choice
- Multiple stimuli
- Free operant
- Caregiver interview

Personal nomination is one type of preference assessment. When this method is used a participant chooses from items that are provided by a person in authority. This list is usually based on materials available to the leisure provider.

> For example, if the agency has a game room, fitness facility, and kitchen but does not have a swimming pool, the list will include the games in the game room, using the available equipment in the fitness center, and the materials and supplied in the kitchen but not aquatic activities.

Another type of preference assessment is identified as *single stimulus*. In this type of assessment, the participant is given the opportunity to play with or manipulate an item. The person is observed and the amount of time the individual engages with the item is recorded. Once the person stops manipulating or playing with the item, the individual is given another item and the length of time the person engages with that item is recorded. Items continue to be offered in this manner. The length of time is then used as an indicator of preference with those items with which a person played or manipulated for the longest duration being identified as the "most preferred."

Paired choice, also called "paired stimuli," is another type of preference assessment. In the paired choice assessment, approximately 10 items are identified that a participant might enjoy. Next, two of these items are presented to the person, and that individual is asked to select one. Once the participant selects one of the two items, the person then has the opportunity to manipulate or play with the item for a determined period of time, such as two minutes, before being presented with another two items from the array of 10. When all possible combinations of the 10 items have been presented, examination of the information that has been recorded occurs to determine which item was selected most often. This item is considered to be the "most preferred" item. The item that was selected least often is identified as a "least preferred" item.

An example of the traditional paired choice assessment in behavior analysis follows. The following 10 activities are identified that Serena enjoys:

1. Read
2. Paint
3. Play video games
4. Watch video shows
5. Bike
6. Talk with a friend
7. Swim
8. Play basketball
9. Go for walks
10. Hike

Serena's preferences are determined by asking her to choose between two activities. The service provider can do this by saying, "Reading or art? Please choose one." As these options are presented, a book and paintbrush might be presented to Serena. Once she makes a selection, Serena is permitted to engage in the activity for a specified amount of time. The following table depicts the various pairs that are offered to Serena.

	Read	Paint	Vgame	Vshow	Bike	Talk	Swim	B-ball	Walk	Hike
Read		1&2	1&3	1&4	1&5	1&6	1&7	1&8	1&9	1&10
Paint			2&3	2&4	2&5	2&6	2&7	2&8	2&9	2&10
Vshow				3&4	3&5	3&6	3&7	3&8	3&9	3&10
Vgame					4&5	4&6	4&7	4&8	4&9	4&10
Bike						5&6	5&7	5&8	5&9	5&10
Talk							6&7	6&8	6&9	6&10
Swim								7&8	7&9	7&10
B-ball									8&9	8&10
Walk										9&10
Hike										

A *multiple stimuli* assessment is another type of preference assessment that can be used. The multiple stimuli assessment involves presenting the participant with an array of three or more items simultaneously. The person is then directed to "Please choose one." Once the participant selects an item, that person can play or interact with the item for a determined period of time, such as two minutes. There are two options when implementing a multiple stimuli preference assessment.

The first option is *multiple stimuli without replacement* that involves reducing the array of 10 items to an array of nine after the first item is selected. The item that was selected is the one that is removed form the possible options. Next, the service provider says, "Please choose one." The person makes a selection and then, again, has the opportunity to interact with the item for a determined period of time. At this point, the selected item is removed leaving eight items as possible options. This process continues until all but one item have been selected. The first item selected out of the ten becomes the "most preferred" item and the one remaining item at the end of the process is identified as the "least preferred" item.

The second type of multiple stimuli preference assessment is called *multiple stimuli with replacement*. This procedure involves presenting three items to the person and saying, "Please choose one." The person selects the item and then plays with that item for a period of time. The service provider then again presents the item the person selected accompanied by three different items. This process is repeated until all items have been compared. The item chosen most often is identified as the "most preferred" item and the one chosen least often or not at all is identified as the "least preferred."

The final type of preference assessment is called *free operant*. With this assessment, the participant is escorted around a room containing many items. The person is then permitted to engage or play with any of the items in the room while the individual is observed. As the participant engages with a particular object, the item with which the person engages or plays is recorded along with the duration of the person's interaction with the item.

The five preference assessments described previously use a similar process to determine a person's interests.

- **SELECT** items that a person might enjoy or prefer.
- **COMPARE** items to each other.
- **DETERMINE** the high preferred and low preferred items or activities.

Now that you know about preference assessments, try to complete the following activities.

Identify 10 recreation activities.

1. _____

2. _____

3. _____

4. _____

5. _____

6. _____

7. _____

8. _____

9. _____

10. _____

Describe how these 10 activities are compared during a **single stimulus assessment**.

_____

_____

_____

Describe how these 10 activities are compared during a **paired choice assessment**.

_____

_____

_____

Describe how these 10 activities are compared during a **multiple stimuli without replacement** *assessment*.

_____

_____

_____

As you reflect on the responses to the previous questions, ask yourself the following questions:

- Did you consider how long a participant engaged with each selected item on the list for single stimuli?
- Did you compare two items at a time on the paired-choice assessment?
- Did you have all items present during the multiple stimuli assessment?

If individuals have an extremely difficult time communicating their preferences as a result of a variety of conditions including severe disabilities, there is another way to collect information that may be indicative of their preferences. A preference assessment can involve a *caregiver interview*. For instance, some service providers use the Reinforcement Assessment for Individuals with Severe Disabilities (RAISD). In this interview, the caregiver is asked questions about what an individual enjoys. The caregiver is guided through questions similar to the following: "Sometimes people like to play with objects that make noise, does your loved one have any favorite toys that make noise?" In addition to sounds, the caregiver is asked about visual effects, smells, tastes, textures, movements, activities, and materials that might be enjoyable.

Other questions similar to those contained in the RAISD include:

- Some people prefer to play with objects that light up; does your loved one have any favorite toys that light up?
- Some people like the smell of citrus, lilacs, or bread baking; does your loved one like any specific fragrance?
- Some people prefer salty foods to sweet foods; what kinds of flavors does your loved one prefer?
- Some people like to cuddle with soft toys while others like toys that are squishy; are there any textures that your loved one prefers?
- Some people prefer activities that have them spin around while others prefer activities that involve rocking; are there any movements that your loved one prefers?
- Some people enjoy repeating the same activities many times in a day; are there any activities that your loved one prefers to repeat?
- Some people like materials such as Play Dough™, glitter, glue, and bubbles; are there any materials that your loved one enjoys manipulating?

The use of a caregiver interview is designed to access the opinions of people close to an individual who is encountering major challenges is expressive communication. Although this type of assessment should not replace attempts at working with the participants to try to assess preferences, it is a helpful way to supplement information that can be obtained from the individual.

In this chapter we discussed several ways that can be used to assess an individual's preferences. To summarize, preference assessment involves the following:

1. **ASKING** participants and family members about preferences.
2. **OBSERVING** participant's patterns of engagement with leisure items.
3. **COMPARING** preferences to determine most preferred activities.

Please go to the next page and test your knowledge of preference assessments.

Test Your Knowledge of Assessing Preferences

1. The term used to describe the means to rank activities or items based on their desirability is:

   a. functional skills appraisal.
   b. needs evaluation.
   c. performance analysis.
   d. popularity scaling.
   e. preference assessment.

2. A preference assessment is used to identify:

   a. desirable recreation activities.
   b. leisure interests.
   c. preferred community locations.
   d. items to be used as reinforcement.
   e. all of the above.

3. Takashi is led into a room with a variety of recreation materials, and Baxter, the service provider, says, "Please choose one." This is an example of which preference assessment?

   a. Free operant
   b. Multiple stimuli
   c. Paired stimuli
   d. Personal nomination
   e. Single stimulus

4. Ten different musical instruments are presented to Pharrel and he is asked to "Please choose one." This is an example which preference assessment?

   a. Free operant
   b. Multiple stimuli
   c. Paired stimuli
   d. Personal nomination
   e. Reinforcement survey

5. Venus is given a sports equipment item such as a tennis racquet, and the amount of time she engages with the racquet is recorded. When Venus stops manipulating or interacting with that racquet, she is given another item such as a soccer ball. This is an example of which preference assessment?

   a. Free operant
   b. Multiple stimuli
   c. Paired stimuli
   d. Reinforcement survey
   e. Single stimulus

6. Aliko is presented with 10 pieces of recreation equipment simultaneously and is asked to "Please choose one." This is an example of which preference assessment?

   a. Free operant
   b. Multiple stimuli
   c. Paired stimuli
   d. Personal nomination
   e. Reinforcement survey

7. Ten art supplies are presented to Kristen, two at a time. This is an example of which type of preference assessment?

   a. Free operant
   b. Multiple stimuli
   c. Paired stimuli
   d. Personal nomination
   e. Single stimulus

8. Which of the following is an example of acquiescence?

   a. Amy does not respond in fear of being punished.
   b. Amy responds by saying "no" to all questions, thinking that the leisure service professional wants her to select only one.
   c. Amy responds by saying "no" to some questions, thinking that the leisure service professional wants her to make a choice.
   d. Amy responds by saying "yes" to all questions, thinking that the leisure service professional wants her to select all of the options.
   e. Amy responds by saying "yes" to some questions, thinking that the leisure service professional wants her to make a choice.

9. Conducting a preference assessment to determine if Faye would like to go horseback riding at an agency that does not have access to a barn is a problem when using which type of preference assessment?

   a. Free operant
   b. Multiple stimuli
   c. Paired stimuli
   d. Personal nomination
   e. Single stimulus

10. Salina takes Massimo to a park and watches him play in different areas and records what he does and how long in engages in various activities. This is an example of which type of preference assessment?

    a. Free operant
    b. Multiple stimuli
    c. Paired stimuli
    d. Personal nomination
    e. Single stimulus

11. Steven escorts Kay to a swimming pool and records the duration that she remains swimming in the pool. This is an example of which type of preference assessment?

    a. Free operant
    b. Multiple stimuli
    c. Paired stimuli
    d. Personal nomination
    e. Single stimulus

12. Holly asks the children of Natasha, a resident in a nursing home, if Natasha prefers spending time inside or outside. This is an example of which type of preference assessment?

    a. Free operant
    b. Multiple stimuli
    c. Paired stimuli
    d. Personal nomination
    e. Reinforcement survey

13. Ramah asks William if he would like to swim with a noodle or inner tube. This is an example of which type of preference assessment?

    a. Free operant
    b. Multiple stimuli
    c. Paired stimuli
    d. Reinforcement survey
    e. Single stimulus

14. Jorge asks Emmanuelle if he would rather go to a restaurant or a movie on a Saturday night. This is an example of which type of preference assessment?

    a. Free operant
    b. Multiple stimuli
    c. Paired stimuli
    d. Personal nomination
    e. Single stimulus

15. Ten books are shown to Roberto at the same time and he is asked to "choose one." This process occurs during which type of preference assessment?

    a. Free operant
    b. Multiple stimuli
    c. Paired stimuli
    d. Personal nomination
    e. Single stimulus

Now that you have completed the evaluation, please check your answers with the ones in the back of the book. If needed, review the material on assessing preferences and try the evaluation again. When you are satisfied with your acquisition of the information and understand your errors, turn the page and begin work on the next chapter.

6 SEQUENCE ANALYSIS

The basis of the behavior analysis approach is the belief that behavior is primarily influenced by environmental agents. **Behavior** is learned; it is not inherent. If behavior is learned, it is able to be altered or modified by additional learning.

The goal of a behavior analysis program is to alter the target behavior. However, that is not possible if the program focuses on the target behavior only, as if it were an isolated event independent of **environmental conditions and influences**. Attempting to modify behavior without benefit of any knowledge related to environmental conditions is difficult. Recognition and understanding of environmental events that influence the target behavior is extremely helpful. Because manipulation of environmental events is a fundamental aspect of behavioral analysis, knowledge of which events or conditions to manipulate is necessary for success. Thus, assessment of events that occur prior to and following the target behavior is as important as accurate description and observation of the target behavior itself.

Those events that occur prior to the target behavior, and in some way influence the behavior, are termed *antecedent conditions*. These conditions could include such factors as where the antecedent events occurred, when they occurred, who was present at their occurrence, and what activities and incidents transpired before the target behavior occurred. If the antecedent conditions or events are capable of manipulation, then the potential exists for the modification of the target behavior.

> For example, if the behavior of hitting others is demonstrated by Silvia while playing softball, it may be useful to identify possible antecedent conditions. Upon examination, the service provider, Ming, observes that Silvia begins to hit others after another player, Stell, calls her names. To prevent Silvia from hitting other players, the leader may take the following two actions: (a) tell Silvia prior to each game that the first time Stell calls her a name to immediately inform the leader, and (b) speak with Stell and explain the ramifications of his actions.

> Conversely, another player, Turner, is observed who does not smile during the entire softball game. Ming observes him closely during a game and notices he frequently fails when batting (striking out) and when fielding (dropping the ball). To encourage smiling during softball, Ming establishes practice sessions to enhance Turner's softball skills.

Characteristics of antecedents include that they:

- Occur prior to the target behavior
- Prevent or encourage behaviors

Those events that occur after the target behavior has been exhibited, and in some way are influenced by or related to the behavior are termed *consequences*. It is important to determine the precise relationship between a consequence and the target behavior.

The behavior can be modified only if the consequence follows each occurrence of the target behavior and is not present at other times; that is, it is not independent of the target behavior. If the consequence does not consistently follow the target behavior, manipulation of the consequence will not result in any orderly modification of the target behavior.

If a consequence consistently follows the occurrence of the target behavior and if it is not otherwise present, it is said to be *contingent*. Contingent consequences lend themselves to manipulation and, thus, to modification of the target behavior.

> For example, if successfully defining leisure in a leisure education class is followed by the pleasant consequence of a smile, then ensuring the presence of the consequence will ENCOURAGE the future occurrence of the behavior. Conversely, if talking out of turn is followed by an unpleasant consequence such as a professional ignoring the person, then ensuring the presence of the consequence will DISCOURAGE the future occurrence of the behavior.

Characteristics of consequences include that they:

• Occur after the target behavior
• Encourage or discourage likelihood of future behaviors

On the following page is an exercise related to antecedents, behaviors, and consequences. Please follow the directions.

After the recreation resource session was over, participants were required to return the recreation equipment they used to its original location. When the time came to return the equipment, Gloria pounded her fists on the ground, kicked her toys, and screamed. The leader of the recreation resource session would calm her down by singing her a song. Gloria's crying and screaming would eventually stop.

1. What were Gloria's behavior, the antecedent, and consequence of the behavior?

   ANTECEDENT: _____

   BEHAVIOR: _____

   CONSEQUENCE: _____

2. What were the leader's behavior, the antecedent, and consequence of the behavior?

   ANTECEDENT: _____

   BEHAVIOR: _____

   CONSEQUENCE: _____

   If your answer looks like the information presented on the next page, you are doing fine.

1. Antecedent: The recreation resource session ended.

    Behavior: Gloria screamed and kicked her toys.

    Consequence: The recreation leader sang to Gloria.

2. Antecedent: Gloria screamed and kicked her toys.

    Behavior: The recreation leader sang to Gloria.

    Consequence: Gloria's screaming stopped.

Notice that in the example, each person's behavior affected the others. It is also important to note that the first example focused on Gloria's behavior while the second example concentrated on the behavior of the recreation leader. These examples illustrate the behavior that all people (even recreation professionals) are continuously modified by the behaviors of the people they encounter.

In summary, the **antecedent** occurs before a behavior, and the **consequence** follows the behavior. **Behaviors** can be prevented or encouraged by manipulation of the antecedent or consequence. The result is an increase or decrease in the likelihood of the behavior occurring in the future.

Now that you have completed the exercise on examining antecedents and consequences of behaviors, please go to the next page and evaluate your knowledge of this material.

Test Your Knowledge of Sequence Analysis

1. What is the term that describes the event that follows a behavior?

   a. antecedent
   b. behavior
   c. consequence
   d. punisher
   e. reinforcement

2. What is the word that is used to describe the event that occurs before a behavior?

   a. antecedent
   b. behavior
   c. consequence
   d. punisher
   e. reinforcement

3. What should you manipulate if you would like to prevent or encourage a behavior?

   a. antecedent
   b. behavior
   c. consequence
   d. punisher
   e. reinforce

4. Eric was watching television when a staff member told him to go the gymnasium. While walking to the gym, Eric pushed Daewon to the ground. After reaching the gym, Daewon reported the incident. Eric said he was wrong and apologized to Daewon. What was the antecedent condition to Daewon being pushed to the ground?

   a. being cued to go to the gym
   b. receiving an apology from Eric
   c. reporting the incident
   d. walking to the gym
   e. watching television

   Directions: Based on the information from the following paragraph, answer the next two associated questions.

   Marcie is at a picnic in the park and wanders from the group. The leisure service provider, Antwon, finds her and tells her she should not leave the group and returns Marcie to the group. After a short while, Marcie wanders off again. Antwon finds her and requires her to pick up trash. Marcie again wanders off. When Antwon finally finds her, Marcie is sent to the bus where she must wait until it is time to return from the picnic.

5. What was the first consequence of Marcie's problem behavior?

   a. attending a picnic in the park
   b. confined to the bus
   c. picking up trash
   d. returning home
   e. verbal reprimands

6. What was the second consequence of Marcie's problem behavior?

    a. attending a picnic in the park
    b. confined to the bus
    c. picking up trash
    d. returning home
    e. verbal reprimand

Directions: Based on the information from the following two paragraphs, answer the two associated questions.

Gulzar has exhibited some aggressive behaviors after attending the first few programs. When cued to participate in activities, Gulzar begins to swing his arms and kick the nearest chair. Each time he does this, the recreation leader comes to him and coaxes him to the group. Gulzar swung his arms and kicked on the average of seven times each session. A program was initiated where Gulzar was given verbal praise every time he came to an activity after being told only once. If, when asked to participate in an activity, he began swinging his arms and kicking, he was required to stand in the corner for five minutes.

7. After the program was initiated, what was the antecedent of the desired behavior?

    a. coaxed by recreation leader
    b. cued to participate
    c. swinging his arms and kicking
    d. standing in the comer for five minutes
    e. reinforced with verbal praise

8. Before the program was initiated, what was the consequence of the problem behavior?

    a. Gulzar came to the activity.
    b. Gulzar swung his arms.
    c. Gulzar was coaxed by the leader.
    d. Gulzar was cued to participate.
    e. Gulzar was required to stand in the corner.

Directions: Based on the information in the next paragraph, answer the three associated questions.

Felipe frequently forgot about his leisure education class. He was usually reminded by his mother to attend. Often he arrived at the recreation center late and had to wait for a break in the discussion before joining the group. For his birthday, Felipe's father gave him a watch. Now Felipe looks at his watch and arrives on time to his class.

9. What was the antecedent to Felipe going to leisure education class before he received the watch?

    a. He forgot about the class.
    b. He looked at his watch.
    c. He was late for class.
    d. His father gave him a watch.
    e. His mother reminded him to go.

10. What was the consequence of him arriving late to class?

    a. He attended class.
    b. He had to wait to participate.
    c. He left for the recreation center.
    d. His father gave him a watch.
    e. His mother reminded him to go.

11. What is the antecedent to Filipe now arriving on time?

    a. being reminded to attend
    b. having to wait to participate
    c. forgetting to go to class
    d. looking at his watch
    e. receiving the watch

12. Behavior analysis is based on the belief that:

    a. behavior is learned.
    b. behavior is primarily influenced by genetic rather than environmental factors.
    c. environmental agents have little influence on behavior.
    d. environmental conditions should be ignored when an individual's behavior is assessed.
    e. individuals cannot be accountable for their own behavior.

13. A leisure service professional can best apply behavioral analysis techniques by:

    a. concentrating on behaviors that are independent of environmental influences.
    b. disregarding a behavior's antecedent and accurately describing its consequences.
    c. disregarding environmental conditions and focusing on the target behavior.
    d. focusing on the target behavior and its antecedents and consequences.
    e. manipulating influential internal agents.

14. A contingent consequence is one that is:

    a. consistently present after the occurrence of a behavior and is not present at other times.
    b. consistently present prior to the occurrence of a behavior and is not present at other times.
    c. independent of the target behavior.
    d. intermittently present after the occurrence of a behavior.
    e. intermittently present prior to the occurrence of a behavior.

15. The following is the sequential relationship that must be determined prior to the application of behavioral analysis techniques:

    a. antecedent, behavior, consequence
    b. antecedent, consequence, behavior
    c. behavior, antecedent, consequence
    d. behavior, antecedent, environmental agents
    e. environmental agents, consequence, behavior

After completing the evaluation please check your answers with those recorded in the back of the book. When you are satisfied with the knowledge you have acquired, please turn the page and begin work on the next chapter.

7 ACCELERATE BEHAVIORS: POSITIVE REINFORCEMENT

Positive reinforcement is the cornerstone of most behavior analysis programs. It is regarded as one of the most crucial factors in influencing individuals to change behaviors. Positive reinforcement represents a powerful tool for promoting appropriate behavior and is the most commonly applied behavior analysis procedure. ***Positive reinforcement*** involves the delivery of a consequence that makes a behavior more likely to occur more often.

The behavior to be reinforced must be specific and measurable so that change can be measured. It is also necessary for the relationship among the target behavior, the delivered consequence, and the subsequent behavior to be clearly defined.

> For instance, Tania is a young girl who does not enjoy physical activities. Her family has communicated that they would like to see Tania engage in more physical activities because she has low level of physical fitness. Due to the family's concerns, Moji, the leisure service provider, has taught Tania how to play several active playground games. Although she quickly learned these activities, Moji wanted to encourage Tania to participate in them on a regular basis. Therefore, when she was engaged in a physical activity, Moji would provide her with verbal praise. Providing Tania with verbal praise functioned as a positive reinforcer and encouraged her to continue engaging in physical activities.

Various objects and events such as food, activities, and praise can act as positive reinforcers. However, an object is a positive reinforcer only if it increases the behavior.

> For example, receiving a hug for a behavior may be a positive reinforcer for some people but not for others. Likewise, receiving free time for engaging in a target behavior may act as a positive reinforcer for some but not for all; some individuals may not have adequate skills or confidence to take advantage of their free time. Similarly, receiving praise might serve as a reinforcer for some people, but others who want to avoid attention may view praise negatively.

The actual effect the consequence has on a behavior is critical as opposed to the intentions of the person providing the consequence.

> Some additional examples may be helpful in illustrating effects of positive reinforcement. The leisure service professional gives a happy-face button to Sarah after she successfully draws a picture of a tree. If this is continued and Sarah begins drawing the tree more often, the button would then be identified as a positive reinforcer because:

- The reinforcement involved the presentation of the button.
- The behavior began occurring more often.

> In another example, after Clarence hit Mary, he was scolded. However, Clarence began hitting Mary more often. The scolding could then be interpreted as a positive reinforcer to Clarence because:

- The reinforcement involved the presentation of scolding.
- The behavior began occurring more often.

Few people would subjectively evaluate scolding as pleasant or desirable. Typically, scolding would not intentionally be used as a positive reinforcer. Nevertheless, in this case, scolding is a positive reinforcer. An important point to remember is that it is possible for a consequence to reinforce an undesired behavior.

Consider Types of Reinforcers

There are two major categories of reinforcers:

- Primary
- Secondary

Primary reinforcers are those reinforcers that are necessary to maintain bodily functions, such as nourishment or food, air, and warmth. These reinforcers are termed unconditioned reinforcers because they are not learned.

Secondary reinforcers, also known as conditioned reinforcers, are learned. This category of reinforcers is further divided into three subcategories:

- Social
- Activity
- Token

Social reinforcers involve interaction between two or more persons. Examples could include smiling, a wink, or words of praise.

Activity reinforcers involve participation in an event. Examples could include playing a game, going on an outing, or taking a walk.

Token reinforcers are objects that can be exchanged for a desirable item or activity. Token reinforcers have little value in themselves. The value of tokens lies in what can be purchased or traded for with them. Money, credit cards, and checks—items that are used in our everyday lives—are examples of token reinforcers. These tokens are not meaningful to us because of what they are (paper and plastic), but because of what we can obtain with, or exchange for, them. Much of our leisure participation is facilitated through the use of these tokens. Tokens are often used for convenience and, in some situations, one token may be exchanged for another token.

> For example, when people are playing poker, they are using poker chips (tokens) that are cashed in for money (tokens), which then can be used to purchase desired items. A token system may be used in a recreation program. For example, a leisure service professional could place a mark beside names of participants who have recently completed a desired task. After receiving five marks, each individual is then allowed to participate in a desired leisure activity with a recreation volunteer. In this example, the check mark acts as a token that can be exchanged for a desired recreation activity.

More information on token economies can be found in the next chapter.

Reinforcer Categories

1. Primary

Maintain body functions

B. Activity– Participation in an event

2. Secondary

A. Social– Interaction between two or more person

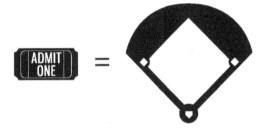

C. Token– Objects exchange for desired item/activity

Observe Individual Response to Objects and Events

Various objects and events may be used as positive reinforcers. For some people, many types of food and drink are positive reinforcers, while praise and attention are desired by numerous others. Reinforcers differ from one person to another. The expression "one person's junk is another person's treasure" is appropriate in this context.

In every case, the selection of an object or event to serve as a positive reinforcer must be person specific; that is, it must be something that will effectively influence that individual's behavior. A delivered consequence is a positive reinforcer only if it works. The question of whether the consequence would serve as a positive reinforcer for the general population is not relevant.

> For example, raw oysters would be a positive reinforcer for some individuals but not for others, while hot, spicy food may also be a positive reinforcer for some but not for others. Praise from the leisure service professional may be a positive reinforcer for one participant but not for another. Remember that the *actual* effect the consequence has on the behavior must be considered rather than the *intended* effect.

The selection of a consequence to serve as a positive reinforcer for a specific individual may take some time to accomplish. It may also involve a considerable amount of trial and error before a positive reinforcer is discovered. This sometimes lengthy selection process should not be regarded as a discouraging factor.

Try this as an exercise. Listed on the next page is a series of items and events that could potentially serve as reinforcers. In the space to the right of the item or event, indicate whether it could serve as a primary, social, activity, or token reinforcer.

1. a dollar bill   _____
2. playing chess   _____
3. drawing a picture   _____
4. a handshake   _____
5. an ice cream cone   _____
6. a blanket   _____
7. a pat on the back   _____
8. going to a ball game   _____
9. a pass to a stage play   _____
10. watching television   _____
11. a candy bar   _____
12. a hug   _____
13. quiet conversation   _____
14. a library card   _____
15. listening to music   _____
16. a glass of water   _____
17. a compliment   _____
18. reading a book   _____
19. eating a hot dog   _____
20. a gift certificate   _____

If you indicated that 1, 9, 14, and 20 were **token reinforcers**, 2, 3, 8, 10, 15, and 18 were **activity reinforcers**, 4, 7, 12, 13, and 17 were **social reinforcers**, and 5, 6, 11, 16, and 19 were **primary reinforcers**, you completed the exercise correctly. The important point to remember is that there is a great diversity of items or events that can serve as positive reinforcers.

Use Natural Reinforcers

Whenever possible, it is helpful to use natural reinforcers as opposed to arbitrary ones. *Natural reinforcers* are consequences that increase behaviors that are directly and functionally related to the task so that when behaviors occur they are naturally rewarded. In contrast, an *arbitrary reinforcer* is one that is not intrinsically related to a task so that when a person exhibits a desired behavior they will obtain a reward unrelated to the task or activity.

> For example, when teaching Yolanda to kick a soccer ball, the leader may try to teach Yolanda to kick the ball so it goes into the goal, thereby allowing Yolanda to receive the natural reward of the ball entering the goal, rather than giving her a piece of candy each time she kicks the ball.

By using natural reinforcers, leisure service professionals can create situations that do not require them to be present when a desired behavior occurs because the participant can still receive the positive consequence from the activity.

Since a major purpose for providing leisure services is to teach people skills that allow them to experience enjoyment and meaningful leisure, there is value in using natural reinforcers that are inherently present in the activity. Also, overuse of external rewards that do not naturally occur with an activity can result in directing participants' attention away from the inherent joys of the experience and instead have them focus more on unrelated, peripheral rewards.

Implement the Premack Principle

There are techniques that can be employed to help facilitate the selection of a positive reinforcer. One such technique is known as the Premack Principle. *The Premack Principle* involves the linking of the behavior to be reinforced with another behavior in which the individual likes to engage. It is based on the premise that the opportunity to engage in a preferred or favorite activity by an individual can be used to reinforce a target behavior that occurs less often than the favorite behavior.

The Premack Principle requires careful observation of an individual during times when that individual has the opportunity to choose behaviors in which to engage. The behavior that the individual spends the most time doing or does most often when a number of options are available can often be effective as a positive reinforcer. Thus, the essence of the Premack Principle is as follows:

If the opportunity to engage in a high frequency or a high duration behavior is provided as a consequence of performing a low frequency or a low duration behavior, the opportunity to do the high frequency or high duration behavior will act as a reinforcer for the low frequency or low duration behavior.

> For instance, each time the leisure service professional, Ida, asks children attending the recreation program to choose the game, in which they want to participate, the children continuously choose the game Uno, which is a high frequency behavior. The children choose this game because they may not know how to play the other available games or may not feel confident that they will succeed in the other games. In an attempt to expand the children's leisure repertoires, Ida employs the Premack Principle by stating that if the children play a leisure resource game which is a low frequency behavior for the first portion of the session, then they will be able to play Uno, which is a high frequency behavior for the second portion of the session.

Guidelines for the application of the Premack Principle include the following:

- Observe when an individual has choice of activities.
- Provide opportunity for a high frequency duration behavior contingent on a low frequency duration behavior.

Consider Implications of Deprivation and Satiation

Use of positive reinforcement requires some understanding of the principles of deprivation and satiation. A consequence that is readily available to an individual is not likely to serve as an effective positive reinforcer. In general, it is necessary for the individual to have gone without a particular consequence for some time prior to its delivery for it to be an effective positive reinforcer. The consequence will have little or no effect as a reinforcer of behavior if it is readily available.

Deprivation refers to the period of time preceding the application of positive reinforcement during which the individual had no opportunity to receive, the reinforcer. *Satiation* describes the condition in which the consequence has been provided for so long or so often that it has lost its effectiveness and no longer serves as a reinforcer.

As an example, a leisure service professional working at a residential camping program decides to use refreshments such as fresh fruit and juice to entice participants to attend a recreation program that is conducted immediately following dinner. If the participants received as much fresh fruit and juice at dinner as they desired, they may be temporarily "satiated" with the reinforcers of fruit and juice. However, if these items were not available during dinner, the participants would be "deprived" of the reinforcer. This deprivation of fruit and juice at dinner may strengthen the likelihood that these items will be viewed as reinforcers by the participants.

The concept of deprivation may complicate the process of positive reinforcement. Deprivation of a primary reinforcer may be an appropriate procedure or it may be a serious issue that has legal, moral, and ethical ramifications, depending on the circumstances. Deprivation of a primary reinforcer should be thoroughly examined from all perspectives before it is employed. Deprivation of secondary reinforcers also requires careful consideration but it may not raise questions of a similar nature.

Satiation implies that, if possible, the positive reinforcer should be provided to an individual in small amounts or for short lengths of time and that it should be alternated with other equally effective reinforcers. It also implies that the reinforcer(s) not be available to the individual outside the context of the positive reinforcement sessions. The possibility of satiation requires careful monitoring by the leisure service professional.

Characteristics of amount of reinforcement include the following:

- **Deprivation** involves withholding a reinforcer.
- **Satiation** involves the excessive use of a reinforcer so that it loses its effectiveness.

You have now completed the information on positive reinforcement. Please turn the page and evaluate how well you retained the information.

Test Your Knowledge of Accelerating Behaviors through Positive Reinforcement

1. Check marks are placed on a chart whenever Molly completes an activity. When 20 check marks are earned, Molly will go on a shopping trip. The check marks serve as what type of reinforcer?

   a. activity
   b. negative
   c. primary
   d. social
   e. token

2. What is the term used to describe the temporary withholding of a reinforcer to make it more effective?

   a. contingency contracting
   b. deprivation
   c. Premack Principle
   d. punishment
   e. satiation

3. What is an example of a primary reinforcer?

   a. eating a carrot
   b. getting atrophy
   c. going to the library
   d. receiving a dollar
   e. saying "very good"

4. What is the best example of the Premack Principle?

   a. If you eat ice cream now, you must eat dinner tonight.
   b. If you go to the movies this morning, you must take out the trash this afternoon.
   c. If you mop the floor now, you may go to the movies tonight.
   d. If you spill the water at lunch, you have to mop the floor after eating.
   e. If you take out the trash today, you may mop the floor tomorrow.

5. Ariana has participated appropriately in all groups for the day and you reinforce her with a token. Which reinforcer might you use?

   a. a trip to the library
   b. one cookie
   c. saying "excellent participation"
   d. two dollars
   e. verbal praise

6. What is an example of an activity reinforcer?

   a. eating an apple
   b. getting a blue ribbon
   c. going to the museum
   d. receiving a quarter
   e. saying "nice coloring"

7. Meng will go outside and hit the tether ball every chance he gets. You decide to use this activity as a reinforcer and let Meng go outside for 5 minutes every time he completes a scheduled program. By the end of the day, Meng is tired. After his evening program you allow him to go outside again. Instead of going outside, Meng frowns and walks to his bedroom. In reference to hitting the tetherball, what has Meng become?

    a. confused
    b. deprived
    c. generalized
    d. reinforced
    e. satiated

8. Two behaviors are identified, one of which occurs more frequently than the other. What is the term used to describe the principle that makes the opportunity to engage in the high frequency behavior contingent upon the occurrence of the low frequency behavior?

    a. contingency contracting
    b. deprivation
    c. punishment
    d. satiation
    e. the Premack Principle

9. A consequence is not a positive reinforcer unless it follows the behavior and the behavior:

    a. decreases.
    b. increases.
    c. is deprived.
    d. is satiated.
    e. remains the same.

10. Zafar has completed all his programs for the day and you socially reinforce him. Which of the following is considered a social reinforcer?

    a. drinking coffee
    b. going to the library
    c. playing cards
    d. receiving praise
    e. receiving 50 cents

11. What is the term used to describe the temporary or permanent loss of an item's reinforcing properties due to it being offered too often or in too great a quantity?

    a. contingency contracting
    b. deprivation
    c. Premack Principle
    d. punishment
    e. satiation

12. What is an example of a social reinforcer?

    a. eating an ice cream cone
    b. getting atrophy
    c. going to the library
    d. receiving a dollar
    e. saying "that's nice sharing"

13. What is the most desirable consequence when working with participants?

    a. deprivation
    b. extinction
    c. positive reinforcement
    d. punishment
    e. satiation

14. Positive reinforcement is the presentation of a consequence that:

    a. changes a high frequency behavior to a low frequency behavior.
    b. eliminates an inappropriate behavior.
    c. is dependent on neither primary nor secondary reinforcers.
    d. is unconditioned.
    e. makes a behavior occur more often in the future.

15. Secondary reinforcers are:

    a. conditioned.
    b. contingent
    c. inherent.
    d. less effective.
    e. unconditioned.

Now that you have completed the evaluation, please turn to the back of the book and compare your answers to the ones provided. When you are satisfied with your retention of the information, please begin work on the next chapter.

8 ACCELERATE BEHAVIORS: TOKEN ECONOMIES

Now that information about positive reinforcement has been provided, one specific method that allows us to systematically use positive reinforcement, known as a **token economy,** is presented in this chapter. If you recall from the previous chapter, a *token* is an object that can be exchanged for a preferred item or activity. An *economy* refers to the systematic exchange of an object for goods and services. A *token economy* then, is a system that includes the use of tokens to facilitate an exchange of goods and services for the demonstration of an identified behavior or set of behaviors consistent with learning and development. We extend this definition to include the positive reinforcement of behaviors that are also consistent with leisure expression and experiences.

The use of tokens often involves a cumulative process whereby a participant earns a token either each time that this person demonstrates a particular behavior or after the person demonstrates a certain number of identified behaviors. Once a person has earned a number of tokens, a time can be designated when the individual presents the tokens in exchange for a preferred item or activity.

Token economies can be used in a specific context or may be implemented across all contexts in which a person engages.

> An example of a type of token economy can be found at many arcades where individuals earn tickets as tokens at different games to be exchanged for a prize or prizes at a prize booth or station. The more tickets an individual accumulates to exchange, the more choices the person has for selecting items, including items that tend to be more valuable.

In this chapter, suggestions are provided to establish a token economy involving a system by which the individual can exchange tokens for goods and services. Since a token is a type of reinforcement, it is important to conduct a **preference assessment** to determine what activities and items are desired by the individual to help with the selection of potential prizes. For the purposes of this chapter, the word *prize* is used to describe the object for which the tokens are exchanged. Tokens can be toy money, poker chips, stars, check marks, stickers, pictures, beads, or anything fairly inexpensive that can be distributed easily. If tokens are interesting to the individual, they can be reinforcing in and of themselves. It is important when identifying tokens that these items, as well as the prizes, are appropriate for the age of the person and that items are not a choking hazard.

Once tokens are selected, it is important to identify prizes. The techniques discussed in the chapter on preference assessment can also be used to identify prizes used for token economies. Examples of items that could be used as prizes include toys or healthy snacks such as fruit; also, prizes can be in the form of time to engage in desired activities such as playing a sport, table game, or video game, and spending time with a particular person. Once prizes are selected, **a value is assigned to each prize**; that is, the number of tokens that is needed to exchange for the prize is identified.

The value can be assigned based on the level of preference for the activity or item and the availability of the item. Highly preferred items can have a higher value than less preferred items.

> For example, during a preference assessment, Sensah indicated that she enjoys taking walks, playing outside, listening to music, and drawing. Her favorite activity is walking on a trail, which takes some time to complete, so this activity might be assigned a higher value of 20 tokens. Playing outside on a nearby playground might be assigned a value of 10 tokens. Listening to music might be assigned a value of five tokens, and drawing might be assigned a value of three tokens.

Once values have been assigned to prizes, the process of exchanging the tokens for prizes is explained. The process of earning and exchanging tokens for prizes follows a **reinforcement schedule,** explained in a subsequent chapter. As a reminder, a *reinforcement schedule* is the systematic delivery of reinforcement for a specific individual. The reinforcement schedule may be fixed or variable and may be based on an interval or a ratio system. For example, a **fixed ratio schedule** means that every fifth time the target behavior occurs, an individual is rewarded. An example of a **variable interval schedule** occurs when, after every two to five minutes, an individual is rewarded if the target behavior is being demonstrated.

The reinforcement schedule includes parameters for earning tokens and prizes. The prize reinforcement schedule will be comprised, in part, of the prize values. This schedule is based on when the opportunity for exchanging tokens will be available.

Sometimes the place where the prizes are located and where participants redeem the token(s) for a prize is identified as a **store**. As such, the times that the store is open are identified as well. A store can be a specific location such as an office or a concession booth. Also, the store can be portable and brought to the individual such as in a mobile cart or a container that can be carried.

In summary, the steps for instituting a token economy are as follows:

1. Use a **preference assessment** to determine what will used be as **tokens** and what will be used as **prizes**.
2. Assign **values for prizes**
3. Determine **reinforcement schedule** for tokens.
4. Establish a **store** for the exchange of tokens for prizes.

Now it is time to try to establish a token economy for Jody. Jody is a 12-year-old girl who enjoys watching movies, reading books, and spending time outdoors. She identifies herself as sedentary and overweight. Jody has enrolled in a fun and fitness program that meets three mornings a week, with each session lasting 45 minutes. She identified the following goals: (a) to become more fit, (b) to lose weight, and (c) to make new friends. Structure a fun fitness program for Jody using a token economy.

1. Identify tokens to be used: _____

_____

2. Identify prizes to be used: _____

_____

3. Identify values for prizes: _____

_____

4. Specify reinforcement schedule for tokens: _____

_____

5. Describe the store to be used to exchange tokens for prizes: _____

_____

As you review your responses consider the following questions.

- Were the tokens interesting enough to capture Jody's attention, but of less value than the prizes?
- Were the prizes something for which Jody would be motivated to obtain?
- Are there a sufficient number of prizes for which she could obtain at different items?
- Are the values for the prizes based on Jody's level of motivation to obtain them?
- Are there sufficient funds to purchase the prizes?

Once the token economy is established, it is time to begin teaching an individual how to use it. Prior to using a token economy, it is helpful if the participant understands the concepts of *quantity*. If a person does not understand the meaning associated with quantity, efforts can be made to teach the person about this idea. Another important aspect of initiating a token economy is to establish clear *expectations*.

> For example, a small token board can be transported with Stannous that says, "I am working for access to the playground, it will cost me 10 tokens." After he earns a token, Stannous can place it on the token board. When he earns 10 tokens, Stannous then presents the token board in exchange for going to the playground.

Therefore, **implementing** the token economy involves the following steps:

1. **Assess** an individual's functional skills.
2. **Teach** preliminary skills.
3. **Explain** expectations and rewards.
4. **Give** token when expectation is met.
5. **Provide** access to the reward at the appropriate time.

There are a few ethical and legal obligations that must be considered when establishing a token economy. First, the leisure service professional should be mindful of the departmental and facility budget when purchasing prizes and tokens. Second, the leisure service provider should *not* include access to an individual's personal items within the token economy. Restricting access to an individual's personal items can be considered theft. A third consideration is that the token system must be fair and just.

> For instance, if a prize, such as a basketball, costs 20 tokens for one individual, it should cost 20 tokens for every individual.

Finally, token systems that can generalize across settings are most preferred. ***Generalization*** occurs when a person transfers skills learned in one setting to other settings, or transfers skills learned from one staff member to situations with other staff members. Additional information on generalization is presented in chapter 20.

> As an example, if Augusto has access to a resource at the recreation facility, such as a gaming system, but will not have access to that resource at home or school, it would be more difficult to transfer skills learned at the recreation center to his home or school.

Token systems that are consistent with what is being done at home, school, or work are desirable and usually more effective. Since token economies involve counting tokens, having knowledge of quantity values, and engaging in social interactions between seller and customer, these economies can help reinforce life and academic skills such as fiscal management and basic mathematics.

Now let us revisit on the next page the example of Jody from earlier in this chapter, since you have already selected her tokens and prizes.

1. Identify one skill of Jody's that you might assess: _____

   _____

   _____

2. Describe a possible preliminary skill you might need to teach Jody: _____

   _____

   _____

3. Specify guidelines Jody must follow to receive rewards: _____

   _____

   _____

4. Identify when you will give Jody a token: _____

   _____

   _____

5. Describe how you will give Jody access to the reward at the appropriate time: ___

   _____

   _____

   Answer the following questions based on your example:
   - What were activities that Jody could engage in that would result in her receiving a token?

   _____

   _____

   - Did you identify an amount of time Jody need to participate in receive a token? If so, how much time is required?

   _____

   _____

   - Did you identify when Jody could redeem her tickets for a reward? If so, when was this permitted?

   _____

   _____

   - How many tokens would be needed for Jody to earn the opportunity to read a book?

   _____

   _____

   - How many tokens would be needed for her to earn the option to watch a movie?

   _____

   _____

   - Were your answers to the last four questions consistent with the reinforcement schedule you identified earlier in the chapter?

   _____

   _____

In this chapter, we learned how to develop and implement token economies. When developing a token economy, the following steps should occur:

1. Use a **preference assessment** to determine what will used be as tokens and what will be used as prizes.
2. Assign **values for prizes**
3. Determine **reinforcement schedule** for tokens.
4. Establish a **store** for the exchange of tokens for prizes.

When **implementing** a token economy, these steps should be followed:

1. **Assess** an individual's functional skills.
2. **Teach** preliminary skills.
3. **Explain** expectations and rewards.
4. **Give** token when expectation is met.
5. **Provide** access to the reward at the appropriate time.

Now that you have attempted to establish a token economy for Jody, let us test your knowledge of the concepts associated with token economies.

Test Your Knowledge of Using Token Economies

1. What is the term used to describe the systematic exchange of an object for goods and services?

    a. economy
    b. generalization
    c. prize
    d. reinforcement
    e. token

2. What is an object that can be exchanged for some other preferred item or called?

    a. economy
    b. generalization
    c. prize
    d. reinforcement
    e. token

3. Manisha needs to earn 10 stickers before she can have access to coloring markers. In this example, the coloring markers are identified as the:

    a. economy.
    b. generalization.
    c. prize.
    d. reinforcement.
    e. token.

4. When establishing a token economy, values are assigned to:

    a. economies.
    b. generalizations.
    c. prizes.
    d. reinforcements.
    e. tokens.

5. What is the process used to determine the types of tokens and prizes to be used with an individual called?

    a. Activity analysis
    b. Leisure assessment
    c. Needs assessment
    d. Preference assessment
    e. Skills testing

6. Fixed interval and variable ratio are examples of:

    a. generalization trainings.
    b. prizes.
    c. reinforcement schedules.
    d. response cost systems.
    e. tokens.

7. If Carlos is given a token for every 10 minutes he participates in an activity, this is an example of using which schedule of reinforcement?

    a. Fixed interval
    b. Fixed ratio
    c. Variable interval
    d. Variable time
    e. Variable ratio

8. Maria is given a sticker once every 8-10 minutes that she plays cooperatively with other children. This is an example of using which schedule of reinforcement?

    a. Fixed interval
    b. Fixed ratio
    c. Variable interval
    d. Variable time
    e. Variable ratio

9. Drew receives a "behavior buck" after every two to four times he initiates a recreation activity. This is an example of which schedule of reinforcement?

    a. Fixed interval
    b. Fixed ratio
    c. Variable interval
    d. Variable time
    e. Variable ratio

10. Prior to initiating a token economy system, it is helpful if participants understand which concept?

    a. generalization
    b. preferences
    c. quantity
    d. quality
    e. reinforcement

11. What is the ability to transfer skills learned in one setting to other settings called?

    a. accumulation
    b. chaining
    c. generalization
    d. reinforcement
    e. shaping

12. Tokens are a type of:

    a. negative reinforcement.
    b. positive reinforcement.
    c. punishment.
    d. extinction.
    e. none of the above.

13. Which of the following is NOT a step for instituting a token economy?

    a. assign value to prizes
    b. chain tasks together
    c. determine a reinforcement schedule
    d. establish an exchange store
    e. use a preference assessment

14. Which of the following is NOT a key consideration when establishing a token economy?

    a. participant's preferences
    b. budget of the agency
    c. home situation
    d. school and/or work environment
    e. staff's personal preferences

15. Which of the following is NOT a step in implementing a token economy?

    a. Assess participant's functional skills.
    b. Assume participant possesses pre-requisite skills.
    c. Explain to participant expectations and rewards.
    d. Give participant token when expectation is met.
    e. Provide participant access to rewards at the appropriate time.

After completing the evaluation on using token economies, please check your answers with the ones listed in the back of the book. If you did not perform as well as you would like, try reviewing the material in this section and give the evaluation another try. When you are satisfied with your retention of the information, please turn the page and begin work on the next chapter.

9 DECELERATE BEHAVIORS: NEGATIVE REINFORCEMENT

One concept that continues to create confusion is negative reinforcement. As with positive reinforcement, negative reinforcement is a method that increases the strength of a behavior. ***Negative reinforcement*** increases the strength of a behavior by removing or postponing an aversive antecedent, contingent on the occurrence of the behavior. An ***aversive antecedent*** refers to some ongoing object, event, or situation that is present in the environment and is not desired by the individual. It is necessary for an aversive condition to exist, or have the possibility of existing, for negative reinforcement to occur. When the individual engages in a behavior that avoids or allows the person to escape from the aversive condition, negative reinforcement has occurred. Therefore, the consequence of the behavior is avoidance of or escape from an ongoing aversive condition.

> A classic example of negative reinforcement involved using shock with pigeons. When shock was administered, the pigeons could eliminate this aversive event by pecking at a lever. Therefore, the pigeons were negatively reinforced for pecking the lever, because in doing so they escaped the aversive shock.

Negative reinforcement occurs when a behavior removes a negative situation, and as a result of this removal, the person is encouraged to engage in the behavior more. Any introduction of an aversive event as a *consequence* of behavior such as a verbal reprimand is *not* a form of negative reinforcement; rather, it is a punisher. Negative reinforcement results in an increase in behavior, not in reduction or elimination.

Any object, event, situation, or condition that increases the frequency or duration of a behavior is considered to be ***reinforcement*** for that behavior. Reinforcement is *positive* if it involves the presentation of a consequence that is desired by the participant, after the participant has engaged in the appropriate behavior. Therefore, something that is desired by the individual has been added to the situation.

Reinforcement is *negative* if it involves elimination or postponement of something from the environment that is an aversive event to the participant after the person has engaged in the behavior. Therefore, something that is not desired by the participant has been removed from the situation. In both positive and negative reinforcement, the behavior of the individual is strengthened.

Some characteristics that apply to positive reinforcement are also applicable to negative reinforcement. One individual may consider an event aversive, but it may not be considered aversive to another. Removing an event would reward the person who views the event as aversive; however, another person who does not view the event as aversive would not be rewarded by the removal of the event. Also, a condition may be perceived as aversive for an individual at one time but not at other times. Removal of a condition is a negative reinforcer only if it strengthens behavior. There are two major responses that can be negatively reinforced:

- Escape
- Avoidance

Escape

In the case of escape, the aversive antecedent is presented to the individual. When the person engages in a behavior, the antecedent is removed.

> For instance, when Carissa screams, a response by Javier, the leisure service professional, that removes the screaming, such as yelling at Carissa, will tend to recur whenever Carissa screams. Javier's response of yelling at Carissa is strengthened by the cessation of Carissa screaming resulting in Javier escaping the negative sound. Unfortunately, the inappropriate behavior of yelling will be more likely repeated by the Javier when a participant screams in the future.

Avoidance

Another aspect of negative reinforcement is avoidance. With avoidance, an individual prevents the aversive condition from occurring by engaging in a behavior. If the behavior occurs, the aversive antecedent is not presented. Thus, the behavior is strengthened. If the behavior is not performed, the aversive event is presented. The aversive antecedent can be avoided if the individual engages in the behavior that prevents the aversive event from occurring.

> For example, Zehna knocks over some equipment and leaves the room to avoid being reprimanded by Matt, the leisure service professional. Her avoidance of Matt reprimand negatively reinforces her behavior of running away.

Because negative reinforcement requires the presence, or the threat, of an aversive condition, service providers do not typically use it. Negative reinforcement should not be employed if the same behaviors can be increased via positive reinforcement. However, an understanding of the principle can help the leisure service professional understand why some behaviors may occur and increase without the application of a positive reinforcer.

Characteristics of negative reinforcement include the following:

- Removal or postponement of an aversive antecedent.
- Removal or postponement is contingent on a target behavior.

Try the learning activity on the next page to achieve a greater understanding of escape and avoidance. Following are 10 examples of negative reinforcement. On the line following each example, write the word "escape" if that is the procedure that is in operation; if avoidance is the procedure in operation, write "avoidance" on the line. Remember that program leaders and participants alike can have behaviors that are strengthened by negative reinforcement.

1. At the conclusion of the crafts session, the instructor detains each participant until his or her individual work area is clean and all materials are properly stored. When each work area passes the instructor's inspection, the participant is allowed to leave and prepare for the next activity.

    _____

2. At summer camp, Terran learns that counselors and other camp staff are empowered with the right to issue demerits as a form of discipline. During cabin inspection, an unmade bed can result in three demerits for a camper. After rising, the first thing Terran does is make his bed.

    _____

3. During dance class, the instructor observes that when Glen and Carol are paired, they do not try to learn the dance steps. Instead they spend their time deliberately bumping into the other dancers. This annoys the instructor. In future class sessions, the instructor uses pairing techniques that prevent Glen and Carol from being partners.

    _____

4. In preparing for the community theater presentation, the director requires   cast members to know their lines perfectly. During rehearsals, cast members must repeat a scene until they do it without making any mistakes before she will allow them to take a break.

    _____

5. When music sessions near their end, the leader allows participants to devote the final 10 minutes to any type of music they wish to hear. Because she does not like country music, whenever that type of music is chosen, the leader ends the session a few minutes earlier than scheduled and tinkers with the equipment.

    _____

6. During the first day of softball practice, the coach announces that in the future, anyone who is late will be required to run five laps around the field when practice is over. Eddie makes sure that he always gets to practice on time.

    _____

7. When Yevgeny signs up to go on an afternoon canoe outing, he is told that anyone on the outing who is caught littering will not be allowed to go on a subsequent two-day canoe trip. Yevgeny is careful not to litter on the outing.

    _____

8. Cory, the leisure service provider, is teaching Liana to play checkers. In the initial session, Liana popped her gum constantly until Cory asked her to remove it. Now when Liana begins to pop her gum, Cory immediately asks her to remove it from her mouth and put it in the wastebasket.

    _____

9. During the drop-in period at a local recreation center, children are allowed to play any games that are available. When older boys are present, Virginia is afraid to play table tennis because she is fearful they will make fun of her lack of playing skills. She waits until the boys leave before she tries to play.

---

10. On the first morning of a backpacking trip, Ashraf, the leader, misreads a map and the group becomes lost. The group grumbles about not knowing where they are. It is mid-afternoon before they find familiar landmarks. On subsequent days, Ashraf carefully examines the map before beginning the day's hike.

If you indicated that 1, 4, 5, and 8 are examples of the **escape** procedure and 2, 3, 6, 7, 9, and 10 were examples of the **avoidance** procedure, you did the exercise correctly.

The two major procedures associated with negative reinforcement are:

- escape

- avoidance

Because negative reinforcement requires the presence, or the threat, of an aversive condition, it should generally be regarded as an extreme measure and **used as a last resort.** Negative reinforcement should not be employed if the same objectives can be achieved by the use of positive reinforcement. It is unlikely that a complex negative reinforcement strategy would be employed outside a clinical setting, with a carefully controlled procedure monitored by a group of behavioral experts.

To evaluate your retention of the material presented on negative reinforcement, go to the next page and complete the exercise.

Test your knowledge of Negative Reinforcement

Directions: The following five statements are examples of negative reinforcement. Record the antecedent, the behavior, and the consequence provided in the statement.

EXAMPLE: You pay your taxes and you are not sent to jail.
ANTECEDENT: threat of going to jail
BEHAVIOR: you pay your taxes
CONSEQUENCE: avoid going to jail

1. The recreation staff member begins telling Douglas to put his crafts materials away. Douglas puts away the materials and the staff member stops nagging him.

   ANTECEDENT: _____

   BEHAVIOR: _____

   CONSEQUENCE: _____

2. The participants in a music appreciation activity are disruptive and loud. The recreation leader turns the music off and the room becomes silent.

   ANTECEDENT: _____

   BEHAVIOR: _____

   CONSEQUENCE: _____

3. Before going out to the park, Carol looks out the window, sees it is raining, and puts on her rain coat.

   ANTECEDENT: _____

   BEHAVIOR: _____

   CONSEQUENCE: _____

4. Ralph joins an activity in the game room and the recreation leader stops coaxing him.

   ANTECEDENT: _____

   BEHAVIOR: _____

   CONSEQUENCE: _____

5. When in the store, Gail begins to cry. The staff member buys her a candy bar and she stops crying.

   ANTECEDENT: _____

   BEHAVIOR: _____

   CONSEQUENCE: _____

Directions: Please circle the letter corresponding to the best answer.

6. What are two frequent responses of an individual to an ongoing aversive condition?

   a. avoidance, satiation
   b. depression, escape
   c. escape, avoidance
   d. rejection, aggression
   e. satiation, rejection

7. What is an example of negative reinforcement?

   a. Ross kisses Sue–Sue cries–Ross kisses Sue again.
   b. Steve and Donna sit beside each other–Steve hits Donna–Donna cries.
   c. Sue cries–Ross yells at Sue–Sue continues to cry.
   d. Sue cries–Ross leaves the room–Ross no longer hears Sue cry.
   e. Stephen hits Donna–Donna cries–Ross reprimands Stephen.

8. The result of negative reinforcement is the:

   a. removal of a contingent consequence.
   b. removal of an aversive consequence.
   c. strengthening of a behavior.
   d. weakening of a behavior.
   e. weakening of a conditioned reinforcer.

9. An aversive antecedent is any environmental agent that:

   a. is desired by the person whose behavior is to be reinforced.
   b. is not desired by the person whose behavior is to be reinforced.
   c. is neutral; it has no influence on the target behavior.
   d. will weaken the duration of the target behavior.
   e. will weaken the rate at which the target behavior occurs.

10. Negative reinforcement and positive reinforcement are similar in that both:

   a. depend on the presence of aversive antecedents.
   b. depend on the presentation of a desired consequence.
   c. require conditioned consequences.
   d. will eliminate inappropriate behavior.
   e. will strengthen a behavior.

11. In negative reinforcement, when an individual engages in the appropriate behavior, the aversive condition is:

   a. delivered.
   b. graphed.
   c. measured.
   d. removed.
   e. strengthened.

12. Negative reinforcement and positive reinforcement are not alike in that positive reinforcement involves the delivery of a desired consequence and negative reinforcement involves the:

    a. delivery of an aversive antecedent.
    b. deliver of an aversive consequence.
    c. removal of an aversive condition.
    d. removal of an aversive consequence.
    e. removal of a desired consequence.

13. Escape and avoidance are alike in that both:

    a. depend on the delivery of a desired consequence.
    b. prevent appropriate behavior from occurring.
    c. prevent inappropriate behavior from occurring.
    d. strengthen behavior.
    e. weaken behavior.

14. Escape and avoidance are *not* alike in that escape involves the removal of an aversive condition that is already present and avoidance involves the:

    a. delivery of an aversive condition.
    b. delivery of a desired consequence.
    c. removal of a desired consequence.
    d. removal of an opportunity to engage in inappropriate behavior.
    e. removal of the possibility of an abrasive condition.

15. As a general rule, negative reinforcement:

    a. has a high rate of success in eliminating inappropriate behavior.
    b. has a high rate of success in preventing escape and avoidance.
    c. should be applied as a last resort.
    d. should be applied before positive reinforcement is attempted.
    e. should be applied only as a punitive measure.

Now that you have completed the evaluation, please check your answers with the ones in the back of the book. If needed, review the material on negative reinforcement and try the evaluation again. When you are satisfied with your acquisition of the information and understand your errors, turn the page and begin work on the next chapter.

10 DECELERATE BEHAVIORS: EXTINCTION

Behavior analysis programs not only aim to strengthen certain behaviors by reinforcement, they often seek ways to decrease or eliminate other behaviors that create problems for the individual and other participants to experience leisure. Behaviors that are problematic take a variety of forms and have various impacts. They may include behaviors that are dangerous or injurious to the individual or others, are extremely disruptive for other people who share the same environment as the individual, create roadblocks to efforts aimed at teaching desired behaviors, or are harmful in other ways.

It is helpful to remember that all behaviors are reinforced in some manner. Behaviors that create problems may be reinforced by: peers, relatives, and visitors to programs, well intentioned but ill-informed staff members, the individuals themselves, or other people in the environment. Whatever the source of reinforcement, it is often valuable to reduce behaviors that prevent an individual from experiencing leisure and developing as a human being.

One challenge leisure service professionals encounter is to help people change their dangerous and disruptive behaviors that interfere with their ability to learn and enjoy life in ways that value the individual and demonstrate respect. One way to decrease inappropriate behaviors is through a process termed *extinction*. **Extinction** occurs when reinforcers that originally maintained a behavior are no longer available to an individual. When a behavior is no longer followed by reinforcement, it gradually diminishes. Application of extinction procedures results in a **DECREASE** or elimination of the identified inappropriate behavior.

> Consider the example of Rashad, who constantly tugs on the arm of Tameka, the leisure service professional, to get her attention. If arm tugging is the behavior the Tameka is attempting to extinguish, responding to Rashad every time he tugs her arm will not extinguish the behavior. If Rashad wants attention, then Tameka's response will only serve to reinforce the behavior. Ignoring Rashad's tugs may be enough to extinguish this behavior.

Characteristics of extinction include the following:

*   Withhold previous reinforcers
*   Results in a decrease of behavior

Use Positive Reinforcement in Conjunction with Extinction

When an inappropriate behavior has been selected for extinction, it is imperative that alternative positive reinforcers for the selected inappropriate behavior are not available. Alternative positive reinforcers are reinforcers other than those that are being withheld. If alternative positive reinforcers are not identified and controlled, then extinction is not occurring, but rather positive reinforcement of inappropriate behavior is occurring.

> For example, Sanchez belches often and loudly during a creative arts session, resulting in the leisure service professional, Diane, speaking to Sanchez and explaining how his behavior is offensive. After this behavior persists for several weeks, Diane believes that giving attention to Sanchez after he belches is reinforcing it; therefore, she decides to extinguish the behavior by ignoring Sanchez when he belches. However, after several days, the inappropriate behavior has not been eliminated because it is reinforced by attention given by other participants. In this case, alternative positive reinforcers are supporting the inappropriate behavior and should be addressed.

Extinction is more effective if positive reinforcement is used to reward a desired behavior that can replace the inappropriate behavior. However, positive reinforcement cannot be applied immediately after the cessation of the inappropriate behavior or it will reinforce the behavior that is creating the problems. Reinforcement is applied after the individual engages in the desired behavior.

There are other considerations that support the combining of positive reinforcement with extinction. Extinction alone may result in the weakening or elimination of the problem behavior, but it does nothing to ensure that a desired behavior will replace the undesirable behavior. Positive reinforcement can be used to effect a desired replacement.

In addition, if extinction is employed as the sole behavior analysis procedure, the odds are high that the inappropriate behavior will return once the extinction procedure is ended. Again, this is likely because there was no positive reinforcement for a desired replacement behavior.

Also, when extinction is applied, there is a high possibility of the emergence of behaviors that are reflective of emotions, such as anger, aggression, frustration, sense of failure or other undesirable emotions. Positive reinforcement can be a mitigating force by lessening the likelihood that behaviors associated with these emotions will appear.

Consider Participant Response to Extinction

It is important to understand that extinction of a behavior will occur more rapidly if the behavior was reinforced continuously in the past. Also, extinction will take longer if the behavior was reinforced intermittently in the past. The unfortunate aspect of this principle is that most behaviors are reinforced intermittently and, as a result, will take longer to extinguish. The basis for this lies in the fact that an individual who has received intermittent reinforcement for an inappropriate behavior is accustomed to experiencing occasions when there was no reinforcement for the behavior. Withholding a reinforcer is not sufficient cause for the individual to immediately consider a change of behavior because in the past the reinforcer eventually was available and might yet be in the future. Thus, longer periods of time and numerous instances of the behavior without reinforcement are required before the extinction procedure can begin to show results.

After an extinction procedure is initiated, it is common for the behavior that is creating problems to increase. This occurrence is termed an *extinction burst,* and means that the inappropriate behavior will be engaged in more often, more vigorously, or for longer periods of time by the individual in an effort to receive the reinforcer.

> For example, Yasmin, a leisure service professional, encounters Rob who engages in temper tantrums. Yasmin decides to extinguish the tantrums by ignoring them. It is quite likely that the tantrums will initially increase in duration and intensity. If the tantrum increases in severity, and Yasmin, not being prepared to handle the increase in behaviors causing problems, then attends to it, the result is positive reinforcement of more disruptive behavior.

After an extinction program has progressed, the behavior may temporarily reappear, even though it has not been reinforced. The temporary recurrence of a non-reinforced behavior is referred to as *spontaneous recovery.* The major concern during a spontaneous recovery is that the behavior *not* be reinforced in any way; this would only delay the extinction process. It is important that all staff members who interact with a person understand goals for the individual so problem behaviors are not reinforced.

Because extinction is a gradual process, it may not be appropriate if quicker results are desired. Also, there are some behaviors that are not prone to extinction. Behaviors that are self-reinforcing are particularly difficult to extinguish.

Guidelines for the application of extinction include the following:

- Withhold alternative positive reinforcers.
- Combine with positive reinforcement of desired behaviors.
- Continuously apply the extinction procedure for numerous instances of the behavior.

Try the following as an exercise to obtain an accurate picture of the phenomena of extinction burst and spontaneous recovery.

Olivia is a leisure service provider who teaches a creative crafts class to elementary school-aged children. The class is Olivia's first time teaching this age group; therefore, the center director, Diego, observes the class and provides any support needed. On the first day, Diego notices that when Olivia is giving instructions, Paul frequently interrupts her. Olivia deals with each interruption by attending to Paul's comments. Diego decides to observe the class during its next 10 sessions and record the frequency of Paul's interruptions. At the end of the 10 sessions, Diego's notes reflect the following:

Session	Number of Interruptions
1.	8
2.	7
3.	6
4.	7
5.	8
6.	6
7.	8
8.	7
9.	7
10.	8

During a conference with Paul, Diego, and Brenda, they collectively determined that action should be taken to reduce the number of interruptions made by Paul. It was decided to use extinction on Paul's interruptions, beginning with the 11th class session. The plan was for Olivia to ignore Paul, withholding attention whenever he interrupted. Also, Olivia planned to provide positive reinforcement by giving him individual attention after he remained on task with his project for a designated amount of time. Diego continued to observe Paul's behavior throughout the process. At the conclusion of the creative crafts class, Diego's notes provided additional information located on the next page:

Session	Number of Interruptions	Session	Number of Interruptions
11.	12	18.	4
12.	11	19.	1
13.	11	20.	4
14.	12	21.	5
15.	10	22.	6
16.	8	23.	2
17.	6	24.	0

Using the graph below, construct a graph that depicts the information provided in this exercise. Label the abscissa and ordinate axes and identify the baseline and intervention periods. Record on the graph where the extinction burst and the spontaneous recovery occurred.

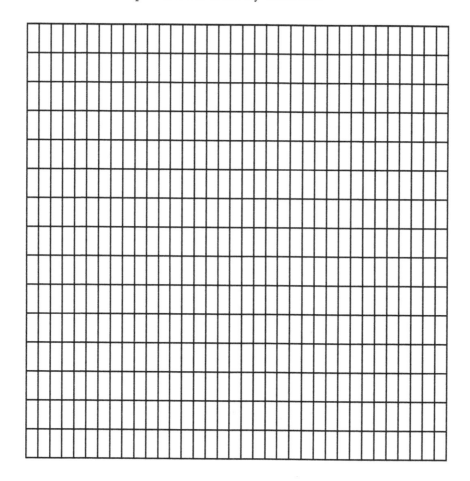

If the completed graph looks like the one on the following page, you did the exercise correctly.

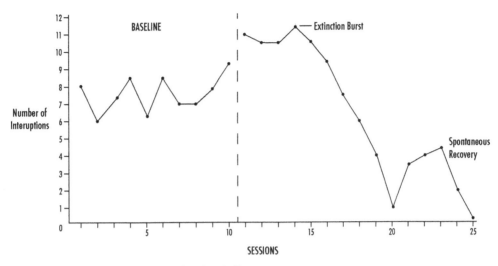

Possible responses to extinction include the following:

- **Extinction burst**: Increase in the behavior after initiation of extinction program
- **Spontaneous recovery:** A temporary recurrence of a nonreinforced behavior

Take Precautions When Using Extinction

There are some precautions to heed before selecting extinction as a behavior modification procedure. Because extinction is a gradual process, it may not be the appropriate procedure to employ if quicker results are desired. Also, there are some behaviors that are not prone to extinction. Behaviors that are self-reinforcing are particularly difficult to extinguish.

> As an example, Derrick, who attends a leisure education class, may spend most of the class gazing out the window. This inattentive behavior is obstructing the potential benefits to be gained from the class, and Rosa, the leisure educator, may want to eliminate the behavior by extinguishing it. However, looking out the window is a self-reinforcing behavior. The pleasure gained from looking out the window reinforces the behavior. In other words, gazing out the window is its own reward. Because it is self-reinforcing, it is not generally susceptible to extinction. Rosa would be well advised to apply an alternative procedure other than extinction to weaken or eliminate the behavior of looking out the window, such as reinforcing behaviors that are incompatible with looking out the window.

In summary, extinction is an appropriate procedure if the following conditions are in place:

- Reinforcers of the behavior can be identified.
- Reinforcers can be controlled.
- Extinction burst can be tolerated by the individual, the individual's peers, and the person applying the extinction procedure.

To determine the degree to which you have retained the information presented on extinction, go to the next page and complete the evaluation.

Test Your Knowledge of Decelerating Behaviors Using Extinction

1. What is the term used to describe the procedure that leads to an increase of a behavior following the initiation of a successful extinction program?

   a. extinction burst
   b. gradual decrease
   c. positive reinforcement
   d. punishment
   e. spontaneous recovery

2. If an extinction program is effective, what will happen to the target behavior?

   a. be positively reinforced
   b. decrease
   c. increase
   d. remain the same
   e. spontaneously recover

3. What is the term used to describe the temporary recurrence of the inappropriate behavior during extinction?

   a. extinction burst
   b. gradual decrease
   c. positive reinforcer
   d. punisher
   e. spontaneous recovery

4. For which behavior would extinction probably be effective?

   a. banging head against the wall
   b. fighting with other participants
   c. inappropriate verbalizations
   d. knocking equipment over
   e. rocking back and forth

5. During social gatherings Alice often approaches people and talks very close to their faces. An extinction program was established for this inappropriate behavior. If this program is effective, what will you most likely observe immediately following initiation of the program?

   a. a burst of appropriate behaviors will occur
   b. her talking too close will spontaneously recover
   c. she is being reinforced for talking too close
   d. she will avoid talking with others
   e. the frequency of her talking too close increases

6. Extinction is a procedure that may be best described as:

   a. applying negative reinforcement to eliminate inappropriate behavior.
   b. applying positive reinforcement to strengthen a desired behavior.
   c. withholding negative reinforcement to enhance the sources of positive reinforcement for a client.
   d. withholding positive reinforcement to decrease or eliminate inappropriate behaviors.
   e. withholding positive reinforcement to eliminate previously unreinforced behaviors.

7. Within the context of an extinction procedure, alternative positive reinforcers:

    a. do not require identification because they are universally recognized.
    b. are available as "back-up" reinforcers if the first positive reinforcers fail.
    c. are positive reinforcers other than those being deliberately withheld.
    d. are applied as a group to speed the process of eliminating an inappropriate behavior.
    e. are an acceptable substitute for negative reinforcement.

8. Within the context of an extinction procedure, possible alternative positive reinforcers:

    a. may be ignored because they are of no consequence.
    b. must be identified and controlled to insure any chance for success.
    c. are used to elicit desired behaviors.
    d. may be applied to effect a rapid decrease of the target behavior.
    e. are always in the category of primary reinforcers.

9. Extinction occurs when:

    a. reinforcers that had previously maintained a behavior are no longer available and it decreases or ceases altogether.
    b. negative reinforcement is applied to lessen an inappropriate behavior.
    c. negative reinforcement is applied to substitute a desired behavior for an inappropriate behavior.
    d. a behavior decreases because it is subject to rigorous disciplinary measures.
    e. a positive reinforcer loses its ability to maintain a desired behavior.

10. When alternative positive reinforcers are not controlled during an extinction procedure, there is a strong likelihood that:

    a. the inappropriate behavior will decrease.
    b. extinction is not taking place and the target behavior is actually being strengthened by reinforcement.
    c. negative reinforcement will be required to support the extinction procedure.
    d. the extinction procedure will occur more rapidly than may be expected.
    e. extinction burst will not occur.

11. When an extinction procedure is combined with positive reinforcement of a desired behavior, there is a strong likelihood that:

    a. extinction of the inappropriate behavior will proceed more efficiently.
    b. extinction will be delayed because of confusion on the part of the client.
    c. extinction will not occur.
    d. spontaneous recovery will be prevented altogether.
    e. extinction burst will be prevented altogether.

12. When an extinction procedure is combined with positive reinforcement of a desired behavior, there is a strong likelihood that the:

    a. identified inappropriate behavior will be replaced by the desired behavior.
    b. desired behavior will be replaced by the inappropriate behavior.
    c. inappropriate behavior will gradually increase in strength.
    d. desired behavior will gradually decrease in strength.
    e. inappropriate behavior will require negative reinforcement.

13. When extinction is the sole behavior analysis procedure being applied, there is a strong likelihood that:

    a. extinction burst will not occur.
    b. negative reinforcement will soon be required to effect any measurable change in behavior.
    c. the inappropriate behavior may weaken, but there is little assurance that it will be replaced by a more desired behavior.
    d. the time required for a successful extinction will be much shorter than otherwise.
    e. spontaneous recovery will not occur.

14. When extinction is the sole behavior analysis procedure being applied, there is a strong likelihood that:

    a. a desired replacement behavior will arise spontaneously.
    b. the client will not engage in escape and avoidance activities.
    c. the client will voluntarily seek negative reinforcement.
    d. the inappropriate behavior will return after the extinction process ceases.
    e. the inappropriate behavior will be eradicated quickly.

15. During an extinction process there is a high possibility of the:

    a. person experiencing satiation from negative reinforcement.
    b. emergence in the person of such undesirable characteristics as aggression, anger, and frustration.
    c. rapid disappearance of unwanted side effects such as aggression, anger, and frustration.
    d. spontaneous substitution of an inappropriate behavior for a desired behavior.
    e. spontaneous substitution of one desired behavior for another desired behavior.

16. Extinction will occur more rapidly if the target behavior:

    a. is also subjected to positive reinforcement.
    b. is of a physical nature, rather than a social nature.
    c. is supported by negative reinforcement.
    d. was previously reinforced continuously.
    e. was previously reinforced intermittently.

When you have completed the evaluation, please check your answers with those listed in the back of the book. If you are satisfied with your work, please turn the page and begin the next chapter.

11 DECELERATE BEHAVIORS: PUNISHMENT

Punishment is another consequence that decreases behavior. This consequence involves presentation of an *aversive* event following a behavior that leads to a decrease in that behavior. It is a consequence that has several negative aspects and, therefore, should be used with caution and only after other courses of action have been tried and found ineffective.

Punishment, like extinction, is a behavior analysis procedure that is used to weaken or eliminate a behavior that has been determined to be disruptive and inhibits leisure engagement for an individual or a group. *Punishment* is the presentation of an aversive event or consequence immediately following an instance of a disruptive behavior that leads to a decrease in the occurrence of that behavior. As is the case in other behavior analysis procedures, punishment should be used for a specific action or behavior rather than for a general group of behaviors. It is an extreme form of an applied behavior analysis procedure that should be used rarely and, as stated above, only after all other courses of action have been tried and found ineffective. The punishment procedure has several limitations and disadvantages, but there are occasions where its use is justified.

It is essential that individuals employing behavior analysis techniques have a clear understanding of punishment and can distinguish between punishment and extinction, as well as identify the differences between punishment and negative reinforcement. Both **punishment** and **extinction** are used to weaken or eliminate a behavior, but punishment involves the presentation or addition of an aversive event following an instance of a behavior and extinction involves the nonpresentation or removal of reinforcers that had previously been available to maintain a behavior.

Although the intent of punishment and extinction are similar, the intent of **punishment** and **negative reinforcement** are opposite. Punishment is used to decrease an inappropriate behavior; negative reinforcement is used to increase a desired behavior. Punishment involves the addition of an aversive event. Negative reinforcement involves the removal or postponement of an aversive event, contingent on the occurrences of a behavior.

Punishment should not be applied in isolation. Rather, it should be an integral part of a well-planned program. One of the criticisms commonly levied against punishment is that it teaches the individual to whom it is being applied only *what NOT to do*; it does not teach the individual *what to do* by assisting in the development of desired alternate behavior.

Therefore, **punishment should always be used in conjunction with positive reinforcement** that will provide the individual with acceptable alternate behavior. It is important that positive reinforcement of acceptable alternative behavior be used in conjunction with punishment of inappropriate behavior. Prior to using punishment, desired alternate behaviors should be identified and plans made to reinforce these positive behaviors. Determination of what prompts the disruptive behavior and what reinforcers are maintaining it can be helpful.

Important concerns related to punishment include the following:

- Punishment should not be used in isolation.
- Punishment should always be used in conjunction with positive reinforcement.

Guidelines for Selecting Punishers

Choosing an aversive event is an important part of punishment. It is possible that what is generally regarded to be an aversive event may not, in fact, be an aversive event for an individual. Therefore, we must assess the individual to *determine if the consequence is aversive* to that person.

The aversive event must be *powerful enough* to serve as a punisher. Presenting the aversive event in a mild form with the thought that, if necessary, it can be applied in stronger forms in the future is problematic. If the event is too mild, it may not be a punisher. Gradually increasing its strength in subsequent applications may result in steady loss of its effectiveness. A better approach is to carefully determine what the strength of the aversive event should be and then present it at that level for its first, and subsequent, applications.

The recommendation is that we select an aversive event that is *as mild as possible* to achieve the desired results. The punisher needs to be strong enough to be effective but, at the same time, nothing is gained by using a strong punisher when a mild one will achieve the same results.

It is important for a leisure service professional to make the punisher *as brief as possible* and *provide minimal social interaction* during its application. Frequently, people exhibit inappropriate behaviors to gain attention. If this is the case, the more attention the leisure service professional provides the individual, the more likely the person will view the situation as reinforcing.

Guidelines for selecting punishers are as follows:

- Must be aversive to the individual
- Must be powerful enough to affect behavior
- Should be as mild as possible
- Should be brief
- Should require minimal social interaction

Present Punishers Effectively

The presentation or delivery of the punisher is also an important part of the punishment procedure and there are guidelines to be followed here as well. It is imperative that punishment is **applied immediately** after the behavior occurs. If punishment is delayed, there is a chance that the person will, in the interim, engage in other behaviors. If punishment is then delivered, other behaviors may be punished.

In addition, the punisher must be **presented consistently** following each instance of the target behavior. Since intermittent punishment is not effective in eliminating behaviors, each instance of the behavior needs to be detected. If all instances of the behavior are not detected, punishment will probably not be very effective.

Furthermore, the person delivering the punisher must **NEVER administer a punisher in anger**. Rather, the person always administers punishers calmly and should also supply positive reinforcers for desired alternate behaviors.

It is helpful to **use punishment uniformly** across personnel because this practice reduces the chance that those presenting the punishers become *conditioned punishers*. A conditioned punisher is anything that is associated with the punisher and becomes, through association, a punisher itself. If the person applying the punisher is perceived as a conditioned punisher, that person's ability to provide reinforcement for desirable alternative behavior is reduced. This is important to leisure service professionals who are trying to create an enjoyable atmosphere conducive for learning skills. If the practitioner administers punishment, participants may develop a negative image of that person. A location may have a similar impact on a participant. If punishments are consistently given in a certain location, participants may associate that location with negative events and therefore be less likely to go there.

Guidelines for administering punishment are as follows:

- Apply immediately
- Present consistently
- NEVER administer a punisher in anger
- Use punishment uniformly

Consider Disadvantages of Punishment

An awareness of the possibility of **situations and people becoming conditioned punishers**, as mentioned previously, is but one of several weaknesses and disadvantages associated with the punishment procedure. There are several additional challenges when using this technique.

Another disadvantage of punishment is that when an individual is punished, the **person may attempt to *escape* the situation in which the punisher is provided.** This escape response is clearly detrimental to engaging a person in a recreation activity and creating an enjoyable context in which to experience leisure.

When punishment has occurred for specific behaviors, a **person may attempt to *avoid* the situation in which the punisher is provided.** In anticipation of the possibility of being punished, a participant may avoid the place where punishment occurred, such as the recreation center, or the person who applied the punisher, such as the leisure service provider. Again, when individuals avoid engagement in recreation activities, it is definitely more challenging for service providers to promote leisure engagement.

If the individual is unable to escape or avoid a punishment, that **person may demonstrate behaviors associated with aggression.** Therefore, an intervention designed to *decrease* an inappropriate behavior may actually *increase* inappropriate behaviors. Any form of aggression presents substantial challenges to everyone associated with the situation.

Another problem with punishment is the likelihood that, with continued use, **a punisher may lose its effectiveness** and punished behavior may return to its original rate. This is especially true of punishers that are not very intense.

Since punishment often results in a relatively rapid decrease in the target behavior, it is possible that **punishment may be used too readily** when another procedure might be more appropriate. It is imperative that leisure service providers view punishment as a last resort in decelerating behaviors that are creating problems for people learning and experiencing leisure.

Because of the aforementioned disadvantages in using punishment, this consequence should only be used when:

- the behavior endangers the person or others.
- the behavior results in significant property damage.
- alternative methods have been tried and proved unsuccessful.

Some disadvantages of punishment include:

- **situations and people may become conditioned punishers.**
- **the person may attempt to *escape* the situation in which the punisher is provided.**
- **the person may attempt to *avoid* the situation in which the punisher is provided.**
- **the person may demonstrate behaviors associated with aggression.**
- **a punisher may lose its effectiveness.**
- **punishment may be used too readily.**

On the next page is an exercise designed to help you review the weaknesses and disadvantages of the punishment procedure.

Each of the six following paragraphs describes a situation in which punishment is applied and a disadvantage of the procedure emerges. On the lines following each paragraph, enter the disadvantage that became apparent.

Situation 1. The dining hall in a camp is an older building with small, narrow entrances. Because of this, campers often stand in line at mealtime while waiting their turn to get into the dining hall. Jerry, an older camper, does not like to wait and tries to crowd in at the head of the line. Claris, his cabin counselor, informs him that because of his crowding in ahead of others, he will be assigned to clean the latrine for the next week. Jerry does not like the idea of having to do extra latrine duty and, while leaving the dining hall, pushes smaller campers out of his way and pushes them to the ground.

_____

Situation 2. A summer playground program has attracted several neighborhood children, a few of whom are of kindergarten age. One of the favorite activities of the children is to play in a sandbox, making forts, castles, and other structures. Cindy enters the sandbox and knocks down the castle the other children are making. Fareed, the playground leader, sees this and begins walking in the direction of the sandbox. Cindy sees Fareed walking toward her and runs off the playground toward home.

_____

Situation 3. The Saturday morning children's hikes sponsored by the nature center are very popular. Because of the large number of hikers, it is often difficult for Greta, the interpretive naturalist, to command the silence that is required when the group is listening for birdcalls. When Greta hears two hikers talking and laughing loudly, she sends them back to the center. This action subdues the remainder of the hikers. Subsequently, when Greta spots any disturbance among the hikers, she sends the culprits back to the center building. This immediately quiets the other hikers.

_____

Situation 4. As part of a leisure education class, Jim is learning to play card games. While playing, he is allowed to listen to music using his headphones. If Jim becomes frustrated with the game he is playing, he throws his cards on the floor. When that happens, the instructor requires Jim to remove his headphones and turn off the radio. This prompts Jim to pick up the cards and resume playing. However, as the sessions continue, Jim still throws his cards on the floor, even after his radio has been removed from his person.

_____

Situation 5. During a free-play period in the gymnasium of a recreation center, the supervisor, Caleb, momentarily leaves the gym to answer a phone call. In his absence, Marcos takes a big mouthful of water from the drinking fountain and spits it on a group of his companions. Caleb returns to the gym just in time to see this. He begins to chastise Marcos and tell him he must wipe the water off the floor. While Caleb is scolding Marcos, Marcos runs out of the gym and leaves the recreation center.

_____

Situation 6. On the first day of tryouts for the swimming team, Melaka and her assistant, Jacob, encounter a large number of candidates, some of whom are unruly. While trying to explain the rules and procedures to the swimmers, Melaka notices that two of the swimmers are trying to throw each other into the pool. She yells at them and tells Jacob to make them stay after practice is over to swim 15 extra laps. The two swimmers are often caught violating the rules, and each time Melaka has Jacob supervise the extra laps they have to swim after practice. The two swimmers begin to avoid Jacob.

If you identified aggression as the disadvantage in situation 1, avoidance in situation 2, too easily applied in situation 3, loses effectiveness in situation 4, escape in situation 5, and conditioned punisher in situation 6, you have a good command of the weaknesses and disadvantages of the punishment procedure.

Because of the disadvantages in using punishment, this consequence **should only be used when**:

- the behavior endangers the person or others.
- the behavior results in significant property damage.
- when alternate treatment methods have been tried and proved unsuccessful.

To determine the degree to which you have retained the information presented on punishment, go to the next page and complete the evaluation.

Test Your Knowledge of Decelerating Behaviors Using Punishment

1. What should occur to the behavior if a punishment procedure is effective?

   a. decreases
   b. increases
   c. is negatively reinforced
   d. is positively reinforced
   e. remains the same

2. What will often occur if people are unable to escape or avoid a punisher?

   a. Their behaviors will extinguish.
   b. Their behaviors will be punished.
   c. Their behaviors will be reinforced.
   d. They will become aggressive.
   e. They will feel ashamed.

3. What characteristics should an effective punisher possess?

   a. brief in duration
   b. consistent, long lasting
   c. escapable, avoidable
   d. immediate, physically painful
   e. negatively reinforcing, specific

4. What is the term used to describe the consequence that occur when an aversive event is added to a behavior and the behavior decreases?

   a. extinction
   b. negative reinforcement
   c. positive reinforcement
   d. punishment
   e. shaping

5. Punishment is a behavior modification technique used to:

   a. chastise an individual for wrongdoing.
   b. strengthen a desired behavior.
   c. strengthen an inappropriate behavior.
   d. weaken a desired behavior.
   e. weaken or eliminate an inappropriate behavior.

6. The punishment procedure involves the presentation of:

   a. a negative reinforcer to weaken an inappropriate behavior.
   b. a positive reinforcer to weaken an inappropriate behavior.
   c. an aversive event to strengthen a desired behavior.
   d. an aversive event to weaken an inappropriate behavior.
   e. physical measures to ensure compliance with rules and regulations by participants.

7. Punishment and extinction are alike in that they both:

    a. are used to strengthen a desired behavior.
    b. are used to weaken or eliminate an inappropriate behavior.
    c. have an element of revenge or retribution.
    d. involve negative reinforcement.
    e. rely on physical measures to ensure compliance with rules and regulations.

8. Punishment differs from extinction in that punishment:

    a. always involves physical measures and extinction never uses physical measures.
    b. involves the addition of an aversive event following the target behavior and extinction involves the removal of reinforcers that had previously maintained a behavior.
    c. is used to strengthen a behavior and extinction is used to weaken a behavior.
    d. is used to weaken a behavior and extinction is used to strengthen a behavior.
    e. uses negative reinforcement and extinction requires the use of positive reinforcement.

9. Punishment differs from negative reinforcement in that punishment:

    a. always uses physical measures and negative reinforcement never employs such means.
    b. can be applied to any violation of rules and regulations and negative reinforcement must focus on a specific behavior.
    c. implies revenge and negative reinforcement does not.
    d. is used to strengthen a desired behavior and negative reinforcement is used to weaken a desired behavior.
    e. is used to weaken an inappropriate behavior and negative reinforcement is used to strengthen a desired behavior.

10. What is a common criticism of the punishment procedure?

    a. It is necessary to use corporal punishment.
    b. It isn't used often enough.
    c. It never works as planned.
    d. It only teaches what not to do and does not assist in teaching what to do.
    e. The physical measures are often too strong.

11. Punishment should always be used in association with other behavior modification procedures. This increases the possibility that:

    a. acceptable alternate behavior will be established in place of the inappropriate behavior.
    b. negative reinforcement will be used to weaken the target behavior.
    c. punishment can be applied as often as the staff desires.
    d. the physical measures used in punishment will not get out of hand.
    e. the punishment procedure will only have to be used once.

12. When punishment and positive reinforcement are used in conjunction with each other, it is likely that:

    a. neither procedure will work because they will cancel each other's effectiveness.
    b. the positive reinforcer will involve the inflicting of a slight degree of physical discomfort on the participant.
    c. the punisher will become less effective and delay the weakening of the inappropriate behavior.
    d. the punisher will become more effective and hasten the weakening of the inappropriate behavior.
    e. the punisher will involve the inflicting of a slight degree of physical discomfort on the participant.

13. In selecting an aversive event as a punisher, it is important to ensure that:

    a. each staff member has his/her own aversive event to present to the participant.
    b. it effectively strengthens the alternate behavior.
    c. it effectively weakens the inappropriate behavior.
    d. it is mild enough to prevent any distress or discomfort in the participant.
    e. it is the same aversive event that is applied in all punishment procedures for all program participants.

14. In presenting an aversive event to a participant, an important guideline to follow is the:

    a. punisher should alternate between strong and mild forms.
    b. punisher should start out in its mildest form and then gradually increase in strength.
    c. punisher should start out in its strongest form and then gradually decrease in strength.
    d. strength of the punisher should be changed at random.
    e. strength of the punisher should be the same for the initial and all subsequent applications.

15. In presenting an aversive event to a participant, another important guideline to follow is the:

    a. participant should never know how the punishment is being applied.
    b. punisher should always involve some slight physical discomfort for the participant.
    c. punisher should be applied immediately after the participant has engaged in the inappropriate behavior.
    d. punisher should be delayed in order to allow the situation to cool down.
    e. staff members should make an on-the-spot judgment as to whether or not it should be applied.

16. A conditioned punisher is:

    a. a second punisher that is applied if the first one proves to be ineffective.
    b. always a physical measure designed to improve the general state of affairs.
    c. one that can be applied only under certain conditions.
    d. one that has lost its effectiveness.
    e. some thing that is allied with the punisher and, through association, becomes a punisher itself.

17. A disadvantage of the punishment procedure is that:

    a. conditioned punishers never emerge spontaneously.
    b. corporal punishment is prohibited in some instances and this reduces the effectiveness of the procedure.
    c. it doesn't work well when used in conjunction with positive reinforcement.
    d. it works too rapidly to allow the participant time to assimilate what is happening.
    e. the participant often tries to escape or avoid the punishment.

18. Another disadvantage of the punishment procedure is the likelihood of

    a. a specific behavior being targeted for weakening or elimination, rather than a general group of inappropriate behaviors.

    b. an increase in inappropriate behavior by the participant as a means of gaining attention.

    c. permanent harm to the participant because of extreme physical measures.

    d. the emergence of aggression in the participant.

    e. the emergence of docile and submissive behavior in the participant.

When you have completed the evaluation, check your answers with the ones listed in the back of the book. Once you are satisfied with your retention of the material related to punishment, please turn the page to begin work on the next chapter.

12 DECELERATE BEHAVIORS: WITHDRAWAL OF REINFORCEMENT

There are procedures other than extinction and punishment that can be used to decelerate inappropriate behaviors. Two additional procedures that involve withdrawal of reinforcement are:

- response cost
- time-out from positive reinforcement

Depending on the circumstances, either of these procedures can be effective and appropriate to use. Leisure service professionals who are familiar with the characteristics of each of these procedures can generally deal with most instances of undesired behavior. This, in turn, allows participants to benefit as much as possible from leisure services.

Response Cost

Response cost is a procedure that may be applied to decrease a behavior that is disruptive or creates problems for a person or group of participants to learn and experience leisure. *Response cost* involves the removal of a specified quantity of reinforcement from an individual, contingent on the performance of a target behavior.

It is an **aversive procedure** in that it involves taking away positive reinforcers an individual has accumulated. Because it is an aversive procedure, it should be employed only after using alternative procedures has proven to be ineffective. Possible legal and moral issues related to the application of response cost should receive careful consideration.

Because response cost involves the removal of reinforcement an individual has accumulated, it is most often applied in circumstances where the reinforcers are in the form of tokens. Items that can be changed for something the individual desires are typically used because reinforcers in the form of something edible or capable of being used immediately might be consumed or otherwise expended by the individual before response cost can be applied.

Response cost is similar to punishment in that both procedures are considered to be aversive and are applied as techniques to reduce behavior that is identified as problematic. Response cost differs significantly from punishment in a major way. Punishment involves the presentation of an aversive event, contingent upon the exhibition of inappropriate behavior by an individual. Response cost involves the removal of a specified quantity of reinforcement that has already been given to an individual, contingent upon the person's inappropriate behavior.

For example, if Marlon in a crafts session disrupts other participants by throwing objects at them and is then required by the instructor to sweep the craft room floor, this is an application of the punishment procedure. Conversely, if Marlon were accumulating points in a system where 100 points could be exchanged for time to play video games and the instructor subtracted 25 points from his total for throwing objects, that would be an application of the response cost procedure. Both procedures are aversive, yet punishment involves presentation of an aversive event and response cost involves removal of a quantity of reinforcers.

When using response cost it is helpful to remember that the procedure involves the following:

- removal of a specified quantity of reinforcement
- is contingent on the performance of a target behavior

There are several factors to consider when implementing response cost procedures. The considerations include the following:

- **The individual must be given an opportunity to accumulate a reserve of reinforcers.**
- **The quantity of reinforcers to be removed must be determined in advance and applied consistently.**
- **The individual participating in the program must be fully informed of the procedure.**
- **It is used in conjunction with reinforcement of desired alternate behaviors.**

First, because the central feature of response cost is the removal of a specified quantity of the reinforcers an individual currently possesses, it follows that **the individual must be given an opportunity to accumulate a reserve of reinforcers.**

> For example, if the reinforcers are tokens, Tameka must be given a chance to acquire a supply of tokens before a response cost procedure is initiated. The accumulation of tokens should not be too difficult to achieve, since tokens are generally used to reinforce weak behaviors, and individuals are generally afforded many chances to acquire them. If Tameka has had an opportunity to cash in tokens for reinforcers, response cost may have its strongest effect because Tameka, after having seen what can be gained by the tokens, should try to avoid losing them.

Second, the size of the penalty, that is, **the quantity of reinforcers to be removed, must be determined beforehand and applied consistently.** The size of the penalty should be determined on a case-by-case basis. Some individuals may require a large penalty; other individuals may respond to a small penalty. The history of the individual is considered, their behaviors are closely observed, and penalties of various magnitudes are tried until an appropriate one is determined. There is nothing to be gained by the imposition of a large penalty if a small penalty is equally effective in reducing the inappropriate behavior. When attempting to determine the appropriate quantity for the penalty, it is ineffective to increase the size by small amounts. Gradual increases allow individuals the opportunity to make adaptations to the penalty. It is better to return to a zero penalty for a reassessment of the procedure or quickly go to a much stronger penalty and monitor its effects.

Third, if response cost is to be applied effectively, **the individual participating in the program must be fully informed of the procedure.** This person must be informed of the inappropriate behavior that has been targeted for deceleration and the subsequent penalty for engaging in the behavior. In addition to being an equitable way to conduct a response cost system, it allows individuals to be more directly involved in controlling their behaviors.

Fourth, response cost should not be used as an isolated procedure. It is more effective if it is **used in conjunction with reinforcement of desired alternate behaviors.** It is possible that the combination of response cost and reinforcement of desired alternate behaviors may soon eliminate the need for the response cost procedure.

Guidelines for the application of response cost include the following:

- Allow individuals the opportunity to accumulate a reinforcer reserve.
- The size of the penalty must be determined on a case-by-case basis.
- Individuals must be informed of the procedure and the penalties.
- Response cost should be used in conjunction with reinforcement.

There are several advantages associated with the use of response cost. Response cost is a procedure that generally **shows immediate results.** There have been many instances where response cost has been effective in rapidly reducing inappropriate behaviors. This attribute contributes to the popularity of response cost as a procedure in applied settings.

Response cost also has potential for reducing behaviors that are disruptive and subsequently prevent leisure engagement for considerable periods of time. In many cases, the application of response cost has the potential for **long-lasting** reduction of inappropriate behavior.

In addition, response cost is a procedure that **can be applied immediately**. When an individual engages in inappropriate behavior, the removal of a portion of the reinforcers can occur instantaneously.

Finally, response cost is **convenient to apply**. It can be applied quietly and with a minimum of physical effort and disruption.

The advantages of response cost are as follows:

- Shows immediate results.
- Has the potential for long lasting effects.
- Can be applied immediately.
- Is convenient to apply.

There are some disadvantages associated with the use of response cost. Because it is so convenient to apply, response cost **may be applied too readily**. It is possible that it may be applied without exploring the use of alternate procedures or not in conjunction with other, more positive procedures.

There is also a danger that the amount of reinforcement that is to be removed, **the penalty, may be too large**. It is true that a substantial penalty may be required to reduce the target behavior, but it is also true that it may reduce some desirable behaviors as well.

> For example, Karma, an instructor, may levy a sizable penalty for inappropriate responses to questions in a leisure education session. This may prevent Melissa from uttering inappropriate responses, but it may also inhibit her from saying anything at all. This would be counterproductive, and Karma would be well advised to reassess the procedure and the penalty.

The use of response cost **may generate other inappropriate behaviors**. An individual may exhibit aggressive behavior toward the person who is conducting the response cost procedure. In addition, the individual may attempt to escape or avoid the entire recreation program. These behaviors would create considerable problems when attempting to develop recreation skills.

As described previously, an individual must have accumulated a reserve of reinforcers. Eventually, **if an individual has no reinforcers to be removed, response cost cannot be applied.**

The disadvantages of response cost are as follows:

- **May be applied too readily.**
- **The penalty may be too large.**
- **May generate other inappropriate behaviors.**
- **If an individual has no reinforcers to be removed, response cost cannot be applied.**

Time Out from Positive Reinforcement

Another procedure that facilitates the deceleration of an undesired behavior is termed time out from positive reinforcement. Similar to response cost, time out from positive reinforcement involves the removal of a reinforcer that results in a decreased rate of behavior. However, *time out from positive reinforcement* refers specifically to a fixed period of time that an individual is placed in an environment that is less reinforcing than the previous environment. The placement of the individual in the less reinforcing environment is contingent on the performance of a target behavior (a target behavior that requires deceleration).

> An example includes the removal of toys for a brief duration, termination of music for a specified time period, or ending an interaction between a leader and participant for a few minutes.

Also, a person can be moved to a less reinforcing environment.

> For instance, the participant is required to stand a few feet from the other participants, sit facing a corner of the room, or remain in an empty room for a brief time period.

It is important to remember that each of these applications of time out from positive reinforcement must occur in response to a target behavior that should be decreased.

When considering the use of time out from positive reinforcement, it is important to remember that the procedure involves removal of a reinforcer:

- for a fixed period of time
- contingent on the performance of a target behavior

There are problems associated with time out from positive reinforcement related to the inability of people to participate in recreation activities during this time. As a result, extinction and response cost are more preferred techniques when attempting to decelerate behaviors. If time out from positive reinforcement is chosen, the following three important factors affecting the implementation should be considered:

- duration
- location
- context

The **duration** of a time out from positive reinforcement procedure is a critical factor. Because participation in the program is the goal of leisure service professionals, it is important to **provide the opportunity for the individual to return to the program as soon as possible**. Once the person returns to the original environment, it is valuable for the leisure service professional to reinforce the participant's appropriate behaviors. Typically, the most successful time out from positive reinforcement procedures do not last very long (5 to 10 minutes at the most).

When moving a person to a less reinforcing environment, the leisure service professional has some options. A person can be moved away from the activity, but this person is permitted to observe the individuals participating in the activity.

> For instance, a person stands a few feet away from participants playing charades.

Another alternative is to allow the individual to remain in the room but prevent direct visual observation to occur.

> One example is sitting in a chair that faces the corner of the gymnasium while others play volleyball.

In addition, a person can be quickly escorted from the room and required to remain in an empty room.

> An example is sitting in an empty shelter while the group attempts an outdoor ropes course.

Often the placement of the individual in an empty room is the most effective **location**. However, it is important in this situation that the service provider **closely monitor the individual** during the time out from positive reinforcement procedure period. If the individual is placed in an empty room, the room must remain unlocked, be properly ventilated and lighted, and measure at least 6 feet by 6 feet.

When considering the **context** of the time-out situation, the greater the contrast between the time out from positive reinforcement context and the original context, the more successful attempts at reducing a behavior will be. Therefore, it is critical to make the environment used for time out from positive reinforcement as nonstimulating as possible. The leisure service professional works to **create a time-out context that is in direct contrast to the recreation context.** It is also important to try to consistently provide recreation activities that are as interesting as possible. The context should provide the opportunity for participants to readily obtain positive reinforcement contingent on appropriate behaviors.

When implementing time out from positive reinforcement it is useful to do the following:

- Provide the opportunity for the individual to return to the program as soon as possible.
- Closely monitor the individual.
- Create a time-out context that is in direct contrast to the recreation context.

It appears useful at this time to attempt to clarify the difference between time out from positive reinforcement and extinction. To distinguish between the two procedures, it is helpful to examine what occurs to the environment after the target behavior occurs.

In the case of **extinction,** the environment remains the same following the target behavior. For instance, a leader ignores the loud vocalization of a participant and continues to speak to the group. With **time out from positive reinforcement,** the environment changes after the target behavior has occurred.

> One example is that, Tashi, a leisure service provider, requires that Cleo remain outside the crafts room for two minutes.

To distinguish between applications of extinction and time out from positive reinforcement it is also helpful to examine what happens to reinforcement during these two procedures. In the case of **extinction** a reinforcer that usually follows a behavior is withheld. With **time out** from positive reinforcement a reinforcer that is already present is temporarily removed.

> For instance, suppose Hannah has established a rule that if participants arrive on time for a leisure education session they can spend the last 10 minutes playing video games. An application of extinction occurs if Peyton arrived late to class and could not play video games at the end of the session. However, time out from positive reinforcement would occur if Amelia arrived on time, was playing videos at the end of class, started breaking rules by screaming loudly and then was required to stop playing the videos for the next five minutes.

Time out from positive reinforcement differs from extinction in the following ways:

- The environment changes after the target behavior has occurred.
- A reinforcer that is already present is removed.

Time out from positive reinforcement and response cost are similar in that both procedures are used to effect a reduction in inappropriate behavior and both involve the removal of reinforcement contingent on the exhibition of inappropriate behavior. However, **time out from positive reinforcement** involves the withdrawal of reinforcement for a specific amount of time; **response cost** involves the withdrawal of a specific quantity of reinforcers.

Try this as an exercise. Following are some examples of behavior analysis procedures used to decelerate behaviors. On the line following each example, indicate whether the procedure applied was:

- extinction.
- punishment.
- response cost.
- time out from positive reinforcement.

1. During a free-swim period, William begins to bully other swimmers by forcing their heads under water. The lifeguard makes William get out of the pool and sit on a bench on the deck for five minutes.

   _____

2. The leisure education instructor brings her class to a neighborhood park for a picnic. During the picnic, Norma persists in crowding ahead of all the others to roast her hot dogs. The leisure educator tells Norma that crowding in ahead of others is rude and, as a result, she must pick up all the litter that is in their picnic area and deposit it in the trash cans.

   _____

3. Campers have the opportunity to earn points by keeping their personal living areas neat and clean. Campers can then trade a specified number of points for the opportunity to participate in an activity of choice. Ellen is trying to accumulate 100 points to exchange for an all-day trail ride. However, she fails to make her bunk before going to breakfast. The cabin counselor then deducts 10 points from Ellen's total.

   _____

4. During softball practice, Sabina tries to hit other players with the ball by throwing it at them when they are not looking. The coach asks Sabina not to do that because she might injure some-one. Sabina agrees but tries to do it one more time. The coach tells Sabina that when practice is over she cannot leave with her friends but must stay, gather the equipment, and put it in the van.

   _____

5. On the playground, James likes to attract the attention of the leader by climbing the ladder to the top of the slide and then start crying, saying he is afraid to go down the slide or climb back down the ladder. The leader then climbs the ladder and brings James back down. The leader soon discovers that James does this two to three times a day. After deciding that James could safely go down the slide or climb down the ladder, the leader pays no attention when James cries at the top of the slide ladder.

   _____

6. In the television viewing room, Ian is watching television by himself. He turns the volume on the set to its maximum level. A staff member tells Ian the sound is too loud for the crafts class that is meeting in the next room and turns the volume down. Ian turns the volume back up to the maximum level. The staff member then turns the set off and tells Ian that he cannot watch television until 10 minutes have passed.

---

7. Jafar is participating in a bird identification class at the nature center. On nature walks, Jafar is given a small wooden disc with a picture of a bird on it if he is quiet when a bird is calling. If Jafar can accumulate 15 discs, he can trade them for a soft drink at the nature center. However, on the next walk, Jafar is talking loudly and otherwise making noise while a bird is calling. The leader takes away three of the discs for each instance of talking and noise-making.

---

8. In exercise classes in the gymnasium, Makayla has developed the annoying habit of asking the instructor to repeat every set of directions he gives. The instructor complies with each of Makayla's requests for the first three exercise sessions, but then decides to ignore all of her requests for repeated directions in the future.

If you indicated that examples 1 and 6 are applications of time out from positive reinforcement, examples 2 and 4 are applications of punishment, examples 3 and 7 are applications of response cost, and examples 5 and 8 are applications of extinction, you provided the correct response for each example.

You have now completed the material on response cost and timeout from positive reinforcement. Please turn to the next page and evaluate how well you retained the information.

Test Your Knowledge of Decelerating Behaviors by Withdrawing Reinforcement

1. Response cost involves:

    a. ignoring an individual as a penalty for engaging in inappropriate behavior.
    b. requiring an individual to cease participating in a favorite activity for a specified period of time.
    c. requiring an individual to leave the premises as a result of engaging in inappropriate behavior.
    d. rewarding an individual for engaging in appropriate behavior.
    e. taking away some of the reinforcers an individual has already amassed.

2. Response cost is an aversive procedure because it:

    a. assesses a penalty against an individual.
    b. cannot be used in conjunction with positive reinforcement.
    c. involves a permanent withdrawal of all positive reinforcement.
    d. involves a withdrawal of all negative reinforcement.
    e. requires individuals to cease participation in a favorite activity for a specified period of time.

3. Response cost and punishment are similar in that both procedures:

    a. are used to strengthen weak behaviors.
    b. are used to weaken inappropriate behaviors.
    c. use negative reinforcement.
    d. use positive reinforcement.
    e. withhold primary reinforcers.

4. Response cost and punishment are different in that:

    a. punishment involves the presentation of an aversive event and response cost involves the withholding of a specified amount of reinforcers.
    b. punishment involves the use of extinction and response cost involves the use of negative reinforcement.
    c. response cost involves the presentation of an aversive event and punishment involves the withholding of a specified amount of reinforcers.
    d. response cost involves the use of negative reinforcement and punishment involves the presentation of an aversive event.
    e. response cost involves the use of positive reinforcement and punishment involves the use of negative reinforcement.

5. For response cost to be effective, it is essential that:

    a. edible reinforcers be used so the individual will clearly understand the impact of the penalty.
    b. it come as a surprise to the individual, thereby making a stronger impression.
    c. only primary reinforcers are used in the procedure.
    d. the individual to whom it is to be applied has opportunities to build a reinforcer reserve.
    e. the size of the penalty is determined on the spot, thereby making the punishment fit the transgression.

6. After determining that the size of a penalty in response cost should be increased, it is most effective to:

    a. allow the circumstances surrounding the inappropriate behavior to determine the magnitude of the penalty.
    b. gradually increase the penalty by small amounts.
    c. increase the penalty in conjunction with a punishment procedure.
    d. increase the penalty in conjunction with negative reinforcement.
    e. increase the penalty by a substantial amount and do it all in one step.

7. Response cost is most effective when it is used in conjunction with:

    a. deprivation of reinforcement of desired alternate behavior.
    b. extinction of other inappropriate behaviors.
    c. punishment of other inappropriate behaviors.
    d. reinforcement of desired alternate behavior.
    e. satiation.

8. Which of the following is an advantage of using response cost?

    a. Individuals to whom it is applied will not engage in escape or avoidance techniques.
    b. It requires no preplanning.
    c. Once the size of a penalty has been determined, it can be applied to all individuals and obtain uniform results.
    d. It is easy to apply.
    e. There are no hazards involved in imposing too large a penalty.

9. Which of the following is a disadvantage of using response cost?

    a. It can generate aggressive behavior in the individual to whom it is applied.
    b. It can only be applied in clinical settings.
    c. It is difficult to apply the procedure.
    d. It requires the use of edible reinforcers.
    e. Ihe procedure takes too long to have any effect.

10. Time out from positive reinforcement involves:

    a. cessation of a reinforcement program because an individual no longer requires it.
    b. moving an individual into an environment where satiation is likely to occur.
    c. taking away a portion of the reinforcer an individual has already amassed.
    d. the cessation of positive reinforcement and the implementation of negative reinforcement.
    e. the withdrawal of reinforcers for a specified period of time.

11. Time out from positive reinforcement is used to:

    a. give leisure service personnel a rest from their duties.
    b. increase the effectiveness of response cost.
    c. reduce an inappropriate behavior.
    d. strengthen an appropriate behavior.
    e. withdraw a specified amount of reinforcers from an individual.

12. Time out from positive reinforcement should be applied:

   a. contingent upon the exhibition of the target behavior by an individual.
   b. in conjunction with response cost.
   c. when individuals are bored with their environment.
   d. when individuals are physically weary from their activities.
   e. whenever a leisure service professional wants to apply it.

13. When considering the application of time out from positive reinforcement, the duration of the procedure should be:

   a. a relatively brief period of time, five to 10 minutes, so the individual can return to participation in the program and receive its benefits.
   b. an extended period of time, at least one hour, so the individual feels the impact.
   c. determined by the mood of the leisure professional.
   d. for a long period of time initially, then gradually decreased.
   e. for a short period of time initially, then gradually increased.

14. When the time out from positive reinforcement procedure is implemented, it is recommended that:

   a. negative reinforcement be initiated.
   b. response cost also be implemented.
   c. the individual be locked in a non-stimulating room, so that supervision is unnecessary.
   d. the alternate environment be as non-stimulating as possible.
   e. the alternate environment be equally reinforcing.

15. Time out from positive reinforcement and extinction are similar in that both procedures:

   a. are best applied in isolation without the use of any other procedure.
   b. are preferred to response cost.
   c. can be applied to reduce inappropriate behavior.
   d. can be used to strengthen appropriate behavior.
   e. use negative reinforcement.

16. Time out from positive reinforcement and extinction are different in that, after the exhibition of the target behavior, the:

   a. environment in the extinction procedure remains the same but in the time out from positive reinforcement procedure the environment changes in some manner.
   b. environment in the time out from positive reinforcement procedure remains the same but in the extinction procedure the environment changes in some manner.
   c. environments remain the same but the time out from positive reinforcement procedure is then used in conjunction with response cost and the extinction procedure does not use response cost.
   d. extinction procedure is terminated but the time out from positive reinforcement is continued.
   e. time out from positive reinforcement procedure is terminated but the extinction procedure is continued.

17. Time out from positive reinforcement and response cost are similar in that both procedures:

   a. are used to strengthen appropriate behaviors.
   b. involve the ignoring of inappropriate behaviors.
   c. involve the removal of a specific quantity of reinforcers.
   d. involve the removal of reinforcement, contingent upon the exhibition of a target behavior.
   e. involve the removal of reinforcement for a specified period of time.

18. Time out from positive reinforcement and response cost are different in that:

    a. the response cost procedure produces consistent results with all individuals but the time out from positive reinforcement procedure does not.

    b. the response cost procedure strengthens an appropriate behavior and the time out from positive reinforcement procedure reduces an inappropriate behavior.

    c. the time out from positive reinforcement procedure involves the withdrawal of reinforcement for a specific amount of time and the response cost procedure involves the removal of a specific quantity of reinforcers.

    d. the time out from positive reinforcement procedure produces consistent results with all individuals, but the response cost procedure does not.

    e. the time out from positive reinforcement procedure strengthens an appropriate behavior and the response cost procedure reduces an inappropriate behavior.

When you have completed the evaluation, check your answers with the ones listed in the back of the book. Once you are satisfied with your retention of the material related to response cost and time out from positive reinforcement, please turn the page to begin work on the next chapter.

13 IMPLEMENT SCHEDULES OF REINFORCEMENT

There are many different ways to determine when reinforcement will occur. The rules that determine when behavioral responses of a given kind are followed by reinforcement are called schedules of reinforcement. Each schedule is the basis for determining when responses are reinforced. The two major schedules of reinforcement are:

- continuous
- intermittent

When using ***continuous reinforcement,*** each of the desired responses is followed by a reinforcer. When a behavior is continuously reinforced (reinforced each time), the behavior tends to be learned more quickly. This characteristic emphasizes the importance of continuously reinforcing a behavior that is being learned for the first time.

> For example, if Denzel, a leisure service provider, wanted to teach Lori the new skill of throwing a ball, Denzel would reinforce Lori every time she properly threw the ball.

A disadvantage to continuous reinforcement is that the behavior being maintained on such a schedule will extinguish rather quickly if reinforcement for that behavior is stopped for very long. The ideal time to use a continuous reinforcement schedule is when a new behavior is being taught. However, once a behavior has been learned the continuous reinforcement schedule is usually changed to maintain the behavior.

Characteristics of continuous reinforcement include the following:

- **Reinforce every correct response**
- **Used when teaching new behaviors**

Schedules that require reinforcement not to be delivered continuously are termed ***intermittent schedules.*** When intermittently reinforcing a behavior, reinforcement is provided occasionally. This reinforcement occurs after some, but not all, responses. The intermittent schedule is more similar to the manner in which reinforcement is usually delivered in relatively unplanned daily activities.

Intermittent reinforcement leads to the behavior becoming highly resistant to extinction. Behaviors that have been intermittently reinforced will decrease much more slowly if reinforcement is stopped. This is an advantage when teaching a participant a behavior that will not be reinforced every time it occurs.

When using intermittent schedules of reinforcement, the reinforcer maintaining the behavior will more likely remain effective all the time. This effect is due to the person not receiving a large amount of reinforcement in a short time. When a person receives a high frequency of a particular reinforcement during a short period of time, the item used as a reinforcer often loses its reinforcing properties and the behavior previously being reinforced will decrease. This occurrence, termed *satiation*, as described in previous chapters, may more easily occur when continuously reinforcing a behavior.

> For example: A young child, Kali, may verbalize at a high enough rate to receive many small toy cars during a short time. Because of the high number of small toy cars Kali receives, they may cease to be effective until Kali has not received that reinforcer for an extended length of time.

Characteristics of intermittent reinforcement include the following:

- **Reinforce occasionally**
- **Used when maintaining a behavior**

The following are 10 examples of different schedules of reinforcement. Find the examples of continuous reinforcement and enter "CR" on the lines following those examples. Leave the lines following the other examples blank.

1. The after-school program at the recreation center includes group singing. Paula, a third grader, will sit with the group but often does not participate in the singing. Before the start of a group sing, Mariana, the leader, decides to compliment Paula on an average of every two times she participates in a song. Mariana decides to compliment Paula after the 1st, 3rd, 4th, 7th, 8th and 10th songs in which she joins in singing.

    _____

2. Richard, a new member of a park maintenance work crew, rarely reacts to efforts aimed at engaging him in conversation with anything more than one or two word responses. The crew members would like Richard to converse for longer periods of time. The crew leader decides to encourage Richard with a pleasant smile when Richard has conversed for an average of 10 seconds. The crew leader smiles at Richard after he converses for 8, 12, and 10 seconds.

    _____

3. Larissa is trying to teach James how to swim, but James is a little hesitant about putting his face in the water. Each time James does put his face in the water, he is given several pats on the back and told he is making good progress.

    _____

4. Alina has signed up to learn archery during her stay at camp. On the archery range it is possible to accumulate wooden tokens for accuracy. When an individual has obtained 10 tokens, the tokens can be exchanged for a candy bar at the camp store. After every third bull's-eye, Alina is given a wooden token.

    _____

5. Storytelling is a popular feature of the summer playground program for young children. The stories are told in an open-sided shelter. Bradley, a kindergartner, is disruptive because he jumps up and runs about the shelter. In an attempt to help the storyteller, the playground leader decides to reward Bradley with verbal praise if he remains seated for a 45-second time period. Subsequently, Bradley will be praised for every 45 seconds he remains seated during a storytelling session.

    _____

6. A basketball coach is teaching his players to shoot left-handed lay-ups while jumping off their right foot. It is a difficult skill for beginners to learn. Whenever a player makes a left-handed lay-up off his right foot, the coach praises the player's efforts in front of the other players by saying, "Way to go" and then adding the player's first name or nickname.

    _____

7. Arthur is being encouraged to initiate conversation with other members of his leisure education class. After every second time Arthur begins a conversation with a classmate, he is given attention and verbal praise by the instructor of the class.

8. Wanda, who likes to chew gum, rarely completes projects in her crafts class because she spends so much time staring into space. Jerimiah, the crafts instructor, believes that Wanda can gain more benefits from the class if he can give her positive reinforcement for staying on task. Therefore, he decides to give Wanda a stick of gum if she spends three minutes on her project without staring into space. Wanda will receive an additional stick of gum for each three minutes she spends on her project without staring into space.

9. Man-Shik, a participant in a recreation day program, rarely participates in any recreation activities with the other participants unless he is coaxed into doing so by a staff member. In an attempt to get Man-Shik to socialize without being coaxed, the leisure service provider decides to reward Man-Shik with individual attention. The leisure service provider wants to reward Man-Shik at differing times after he has played cards and plans to do so an average of every three games he plays.

10. The favorite toy of Betsy, a preschooler, is a huge, stuffed panda. Betsy is being taught to engage in cooperative play with other preschool children. The play leader plans to reward Betsy after she has engaged in cooperative play for an average of 90 seconds but predetermines that Betsy will be allowed to hug the panda after cooperative play periods of 75, 115, and 90 seconds.

Two major intermittent schedules of reinforcement are:

- Ratio
- Interval

Ratio schedules are those schedules in which reinforcement is administered on the basis of a required number of responses that must occur before a reinforcer is delivered. A schedule in which every third response is reinforced would be a ratio schedule because there is a prescribed ratio of responses required for each reinforcer.

> An example would be the delivery of verbal praise after every third time Cindy catches a ball.

Ratio schedules of reinforcement are further divided into categories termed:

- Fixed ratio
- Variable ratio

When using a fixed ratio schedule, the **number** of responses required for reinforcement is **set** at a designated number. This number does not change after each reinforcer is delivered. In the example of a fixed ratio schedule of three, three responses must occur prior to receiving reinforcement.

Characteristics of a fixed ratio schedule of reinforcement include:

- Based on the number of times a behavior occurs.
- The schedule is set at a designated number.

Return to the 10 examples of different schedules of reinforcement. Find the examples of fixed ratio schedules of reinforcement and enter "FR" on the lines following those examples. Leave the lines following the remaining examples blank.

A variable ratio schedule of reinforcement also requires a number of responses per reinforcer. However, the number of responses varies after the delivery of reinforcement.

> For example: on a variable ratio schedule of reinforcement of two, Camila may identify a leisure resource and be reinforced, make three identifications and be reinforced, then make two statements identifying leisure resources and be reinforced, etc.

Notice that the number of responses required for each successive reinforcement changes, but the "average" number of responses required is two. The number "2" designates how many responses, on the average, are required for reinforcement.

When using a variable ratio schedule of reinforcement, the leisure service professional must plan in advance to insure that the number of responses required varies randomly each time, and the average number of responses required is the same as the number specified initially, as opposed to developing the schedule "on the spot." This unplanned scheduling often results in a different average number of responses required.

Characteristics of a variable ratio schedule of reinforcement include the following:

- Based on the number of times a behavior occurs.
- Reinforcement is delivered based on the average number of responses.

Return to the 10 examples of different schedules of reinforcement. Find the examples of variable ratio schedules of reinforcement and enter "VR" on the lines following those examples. Leave the lines following the remaining examples blank.

Interval schedules of reinforcement are schedules that involve the reinforcement of a response after the passage of some specified time. After each specified interval has passed, the next response is reinforced.

> For example: if 30 seconds is the specified interval, then, Bryan, the leisure service provider would wait 30 seconds and then reinforce the first desired response occurring after the 30 seconds. Bryan would then wait another 30 seconds before reinforcing, and so on.

Thus, on an interval schedule, the reinforcement is still response-contingent. Response-contingent refers to the fact that reinforcement only occurs when the appropriate response occurs. With this type of schedule there is a specified period of time that must transpire prior to the response being reinforced.

Two types of interval schedules are:

- fixed interval
- variable interval

Fixed interval schedules of reinforcement denote a consistent amount of time that must transpire between opportunities for reinforcement. The length of the interval does not change after successive reinforcers are delivered.

For example: with a fixed interval of two minutes (the first presentation of the reinforcer would occur after two minutes), the recreation professional, Olivia, would use a watch or timer to determine when two minutes have elapsed. Olivia would then reinforce the next desired response that occurs and then begin timing the next two-minute interval.

Characteristics of fixed interval schedule of reinforcement include the following:

- **Based on a period of time.**
- **The schedule does not change.**

Return to the 10 examples of different schedules of reinforcement. Find the examples of fixed interval schedules of reinforcement and enter "FI" on the lines following those examples. Leave the lines following the remaining examples blank.

Variable interval schedules of reinforcement have a specified time, which varies in length after the reinforcer is delivered. An average interval is specified by the schedule and the length of any given interval varies according to this average interval.

Planning a variable interval schedule is similar to planning a variable ratio schedule, except the random numbers represent interval lengths rather than number of responses. The range of the interval lengths is calculated the same as for a variable ratio schedule.

Characteristics of a variable interval schedule of reinforcement include the following:

- **Based on a period of time.**
- **Reinforcement is delivered based on the average number of responses.**

Return to the 10 examples of different schedules of reinforcement. Find the examples of the variable interval schedules of reinforcement and enter "VI" on the lines following those examples.

Each of the 10 examples should now be coded in some manner. If you coded examples 1 and 9 as VR, 2 and 10 as VI, 3 and 6 as CR, 4 and 7 as FR, and 5 and 8 as FI, you did the exercise correctly.

Any type of behavioral consequence may be delivered on any of the aforementioned schedules. When punishers are delivered on these schedules, the results are very different. A continuous schedule of punishment provides the most long lasting suppression of behavior. With continuous punishment there is also an increased chance that the person being punished will adapt to the punisher, resulting in the loss of its effectiveness. The suppression of behavior is less complete when using an intermittent schedule of punishment, and if punishment is stopped, the behavior will return at a rate similar to the initial rate sooner than it would with continuous punishment.

Schedules of Reinforcement

	Schedule is unchanging	Schedule changes
Based on number of responses	FIXED RATIO	VARIABLE RATIO
Based on amount of time	FIXED INTERVAL	VARIABLE INTERVAL

Please go to the next page to assess how well you retained the information presented on schedules of reinforcement.

Test Your Knowledge of Schedules of Reinforcement

1. Lorenzo is allowed to play cards for 15 minutes if participating in the exercise group for one hour.

   a. fixed interval
   b. fixed ratio
   c. variable interval
   d. variable ratio

2. Marian is given a pat on the back after every two correct verbal responses.

   a. fixed interval
   b. fixed ratio
   c. variable interval
   d. variable ratio

3. Carol is told she is painting very nicely once every two minutes.

   a. fixed interval
   b. fixed ratio
   c. variable interval
   d. variable ratio

4. The leisure service professional smiles at Rahim on the average of every three strikes he pitches in a baseball game.

   a. fixed interval
   b. fixed ratio
   c. variable interval
   d. variable ratio

5. Dakota is given a toy on the average of every three times he follows the leader's directions.

   a. fixed interval
   b. fixed ratio
   c. variable interval
   d. variable ratio

6. Won-Seok is given an apple after he attends the leisure resource session.

   a. fixed interval
   b. fixed ratio
   c. variable interval
   d. variable ratio

7. Sonya is given a check mark on the blackboard on an average of every three minutes she continues to work on her pottery.

   a. fixed interval
   b. fixed ratio
   c. variable interval
   d. variable ratio

8. Odin is told he performs well after every 10 lines he recites in a play.

   a. fixed interval
   b. fixed ratio
   c. variable interval
   d. variable ratio

9. The leisure service professional has scheduled free play at 10:00 and at 2:00 for participants who acted appropriately during social games.

   a. fixed interval
   b. fixed ratio
   c. variable interval
   d. variable ratio

10. Approximately once every 10 minutes one of the recreation staff tells William that he is effectively participating in the leisure resource group.

    a. fixed interval
    b. fixed ratio
    c. variable interval
    d. variable ratio

11. Francisco has enrolled in a swim class. He has never attempted to swim. You set up a program to teach him the new skill of putting his head under water. What schedule of reinforcement would be used?

    a. continuous
    b. fixed interval
    c. intermittent
    d. variable interval
    e. variable ratio

12. The leisure service professional allows Sheila to ring a bell each time she correctly responds. This is an example of which of the following reinforcement schedules?

    a. duration
    b. fixed interval
    c. fixed ratio
    d. variable interval
    e. variable ratio

13. After extensive training, Xavier has learned to participate in a group discussion session. To maintain this skill, what reinforcement schedule should be applied?

    a. continuous
    b. duration
    c. fixed interval
    d. fixed ratio
    e. variable interval

14. The following situation may more easily occur when continuously reinforcing a behavior.

    a. aggression
    b. deprivation
    c. generalization
    d. punishment
    e. satiation

15. Which schedule of punishment provides the most long lasting suppression of behavior?

    a. continuous
    b. fixed interval
    c. intermittent
    d. variable interval
    e. variable ratio

Now that you have completed the evaluation, please turn to the back of the book and check your answers with the ones listed. When you have finished, please turn the page and begin work on the next chapter.

14 SHAPE BEHAVIORS

A common objective of many leisure programs is to encourage participants to develop new leisure behaviors. One way to do this is to use various reinforcement procedures. However, sometimes it is not possible to reinforce the desired new behavior because participants may rarely demonstrate this behavior. The participants need assistance in learning the new behavior.

A behavior analysis technique that can be applied to help individuals develop new behaviors is termed shaping. *Shaping* is the development of a new behavior by reinforcing a series of behaviors that are progressively similar to the desired new behavior. With shaping, a new behavior can be initiated by first reinforcing a behavior that the person already exhibits that is similar to the desired new behavior. As time passes, the person is required to exhibit behaviors that are more and more similar to the desired new behavior in order to obtain reinforcement.

The shaping procedure involves a series of steps. With each successive step, the behavior required for reinforcement has to be more similar to the new behavior being taught than the behaviors that preceded it. Behaviors in the series of steps that were previously reinforced would then be subject to extinction. The final desired behavior is called the *terminal behavior.* The reinforced behaviors that are required to be more and more similar to the terminal behavior are called *successive approximations*.

There are five steps to follow in implementing a shaping procedure. Shaping requires that all persons applying the procedure have a clear understanding of what the terminal behavior is to be. The steps include:

- **Describe the specific terminal behavior in overt terms.**
- **Select the behavior that will serve as the starting point.**
- **Determine successive approximations of the behavior.**
- **Proceed at the optimum pace.**
- **Provide reinforcement to establish a new successive approximation and withhold reinforcement to extinguish a previous approximation.**

Describe the Specific Terminal Behavior in Overt Terms

The first step in shaping is to **describe the specific terminal behavior in overt terms.** It is essential that the terminal behavior be described in observable and measurable terms to reduce the likelihood of possible confusion or misunderstanding concerning what the person is to do. If all people applying the procedure have the same understanding and expectations, then there should be consistency of reinforcement and progress should follow in an orderly manner. It is recommended that all of the characteristics (duration, frequency, intensity, etc.) of the terminal behavior be specified so that all successive approximations can be reinforced.

> For example, Tobias throws himself on the ground when he is tired of playing soccer. The specific terminal behavior that Christina, a leisure service professional, might want to introduce would be for Tobias to signal to the coach that he would like to come out of the game by "placing his hand on his head."

Shaping is a gradual process aimed at arriving at a new behavior. The essence of shaping is the reinforcement of successive approximations.

Select the Behavior that will serve as the Starting Point

The second step in shaping is to review the behaviors of the individual and **select the behavior that will serve as the starting point** on the road to achieving the terminal behavior. The individual must already engage in some form of behavior, no matter how rudimentary, that resembles the terminal behavior. That behavior can serve as the starting point. The starting behavior should be one that carries some assurance that it will occur with enough frequency during training sessions so that it can be reinforced and then serve as the basis for a succeeding closer approximation of the terminal behavior.

> In the above example, the behavior that Christina wants to change is Tobias throwing himself on the ground.

Determine Successive Approximations of the Behavior

The third step in shaping is to determine **successive approximations of the behavior** that will be reinforced. Sometimes it is difficult to decide in advance exactly which behaviors to require as successive approximations. Because the participant's behavior may change slowly in very small amounts, or more quickly in large amounts, the person applying the shaping procedure often does not have the information necessary to predict exactly how much of a change to require. In such cases, it is appropriate to use professional judgment to arrive at an "on the spot" decision to determine which behaviors to accept as successive approximations and thus which behaviors to reinforce. However, tentative decisions concerning which small behavior changes to accept as successive approximations can be made prior to the implementation of the shaping procedure.

> In the example of Tobias in the soccer game, examples of successive approximations might include:
>
> - Tobias touches his head when sitting on the ground; the coach escorts him to sideline where he will get a reinforcer.
> - Tobias touches his head before sitting on the ground; the coach escorts him to sideline where he gets reinforcer.
> - Tobias walks over to sideline and touches his head; the coach gives him a reinforcement.

Proceed at the Optimum Pace

The fourth step in shaping is to **proceed at the optimum pace**. This step requires accurate monitoring of the process and sound decisions based on the available data. The shaping procedure cannot be hurried, for there is a strong possibility that a successive approximation will not be fully established before moving on to the next one. If this occurs, the previous successive approximation may be lost as a result of extinction before the new successive approximation is established through reinforcement. This is a serious obstacle in shaping.

Optimum pace also refers to the differences between successive approximations; that is, the amount or degree of change between the behaviors. Shaping should progress with behavior changes that proceed in a positive direction but are small enough to ensure their mastery by the participant. Otherwise, there is again the possibility that the previous successive approximation will be lost through extinction before the new successive approximation is established.

If the participant is unable to achieve a new successive approximation, it is probably due to being required to move too quickly through successive approximations or to make too large a jump between them. If this is the case, an earlier approximation that was firmly established should be re-established for the participant and the procedure then modified as it moves forward.

On some occasions, when the participant does not engage in the required behavior, it is possible to give the participant a small amount of the reinforcer to see if this will bring about the required behavior, a process known as *reinforcer sampling.* Reinforcer sampling has been used with success in many cases. The potential danger in reinforcer sampling is that the participant may be reinforced for not engaging in the required behavior. However, providing only small amounts of the reinforcer can control this possibility. The remainder of the reinforcer can be provided after the required behavioral response.

> In the example with Tobias, the length of time that Tobias rests might be minimal until he reaches the terminal behavior.

Provide Reinforcement to Establish a New Successive Approximation and Withhold Reinforcement to Extinguish a Previous Approximation

The fifth step in the shaping procedure is one that is done simultaneously with the other steps. The leisure service professional **provides reinforcement to establish a new successive approximation and withholds reinforcement to extinguish a previous approximation**. Every time a successive approximation is exhibited it should be reinforced. Because it is a new behavior that is being taught to the participant, a continuous schedule of reinforcement should be applied. Not only can shaping be used to teach desired behaviors but it can also be used to teach play skills.

> For example, a goal could be to teach Desiree how to stack blocks one on top of the other. The behavior that Marcus, the leisure service professional, wants to change is that Desiree traditionally lines blocks horizontally. The successive approximation might be stacking two blocks, then three blocks, then six blocks, etc. The optimal pace might be stacking two blocks 10 times in a row, three blocks five times in a row, and six blocks five times in a row. Marcus then uses continuous reinforcement until Desiree masters the skill.

For purposes of review, indicate the proper order of the steps of the shaping procedure.

1. _____

2. _____

3. _____

4. _____

5. _____

Your responses should be the same as the characteristics listed on the following page.

Characteristics of the shaping procedure:

- **Describe the specific terminal behavior ibn overt term.**
- **Select the behavior that will serve as the starting point.**
- **Determine successive approximations of the behavior.**
- **Proceed at the optimum pace.**
- **Provides reinforcement to establish a new successive approximation and withhold reinforcement to extinguish a previous approximation.**

Now that you have completed the section related to shaping, please go to the next page and evaluate your retention of the material.

Test Your Knowledge About Shaping

1. What should the recreation leader reinforce when Thomas is being taught the new skill of rowing a boat?

    a. incompatible behaviors of the new skill
    b. previously learned tasks
    c. skills related to the new skill
    d. successive approximations of the new skill
    e. the total task

2. Once a substep has been learned and reinforced a specified number of times during a shaping program, what should the leisure service provider do?

    a. Generalize the learned step.
    b. Go back and reinforce that substep.
    c. Ignore the appropriate behavior.
    d. Incorporate the next step.
    e. Specify the target behavior.

3. You have observed that Susan walks around the gymnasium rather than participating in the recreation program. What should be the first step in developing a shaping program for Susan?

    a. Chain small steps together.
    b. Decide on a criterion for evaluation.
    c. Develop a sequenced plan.
    d. Reinforce successive approximations.
    e. Specify the target behavior.

4. What is the term used to describe the reinforced behaviors that are required to be more and more similar to the target behavior while shaping a behavior?

    a. learned steps
    b. sequential plans
    c. successive approximations
    d. task analysis
    e. total tasks

5. Which of the following is an example of shaping a behavior if reinforcement is given to the participant after each of the following steps?

    a. enters activity room, writes name, is praised by the leader
    b. picks up pen, sets pen down, touches pen, makes marks on paper
    c. touches pen, lifts pen, rests pen point on paper, makes mark on paper
    d. writes name, is praised by leader, participant smiles
    e. writes with pen, writes with pencil, writes with crayons

6. What is the purpose of shaping?

    a. develop a new behavior
    b. eliminate the need for extinction
    c. gradually weaken an inappropriate behavior
    d. improve a participant's physical condition
    e. rapidly weaken an inappropriate behavior

7. What is involved in the shaping procedure?

   a. a series of exercises aimed at improving physical fitness
   b. a series of steps aimed at the gradual extinction of an inappropriate behavior
   c. punishment of inappropriate behavior in conjunction with negative reinforcement of a desired behavior
   d. punishment of inappropriate behavior in conjunction with positive reinforcement of a desired behavior
   e. the reinforcement of a series of behavior that are progressively similar to the desired new behavior

8. What is the final desired behavior called during the shaping process?

   a. positive behavior
   b. shaping behavior
   c. successive behavior
   d. target behavior
   e. terminal behavior

9. What are successive approximations?

   a. behavior modification training sessions that take place on consecutive days
   b. behaviors that bear no resemblance to the final desired behavior
   c. reinforced behaviors that are required to be progressively similar to the final desired behavior
   d. reinforcers that are applied in rapid succession
   e. reinforcers that are somewhat similar to the positive reinforcer being applied

10. What is the first step in implementing a shaping procedure?

   a. Punish inappropriate behavior.
   b. Put an end to successive approximations.
   c. Use covert terms to describe the final desired behavior.
   d. Use negative reinforcement to eliminate the inappropriate behavior.
   e. Use overt terms to describe the final desired behavior.

11. When selecting a starting behavior in the shaping procedure the behavior should:

   a. be negatively reinforced so that it will weaken gradually.
   b. be rapidly weakened by punishment so that reinforcement of future behaviors that are similar to the final desired behavior can begin.
   c. bear no resemblance to the final desired behavior in order to avoid confusing the participant.
   d. not be reinforced so that substitute behaviors can be quickly learned by the participant.
   e. occur often enough so that it can be positively reinforced and serve as a foundation for future behaviors that are progressively similar to the final desired behavior.

12. In the shaping procedure, once a successive approximation is firmly established, what should the previous successive approximation be subjected to?

   a. alternate positive reinforcers
   b. extinction
   c. negative reinforcement
   d. positive reinforcement
   e. punishment

13. In shaping, what should a new successive approximation always be?

    a. extinguished
    b. ignored if it doesn't weaken of its own accord
    c. negatively reinforced
    d. positively reinforced
    e. punished

14. If the shaping procedure is hurried, what is there a strong likelihood of?

    a. A new successive approximation will not be firmly established before the previous successive approximation is lost through extinction.
    b. Alternative positive reinforcers will have to be utilized.
    c. Negative reinforcement will be applied to weaken the starting behavior.
    d. The original final desired behavior will have to be replaced with an alternate.
    e. The participant will have to be punished in order to prevent inappropriate behavior.

15. In shaping, what should be the degree of change between successive approximations?

    a. be ignored because it has no relevance to the participant
    b. determined beforehand and no deviation should be permitted
    c. be determined by random choice to avoid rigid behavior patterns
    d. progress toward the desired final behavior but be small enough to be mastered by the participant
    e. progress toward the desired final behavior in large increments to simplify the process

16. What does the phrase "reinforcer sampling" mean?

    a. giving a participant a series of positive reinforcers
    b. giving a participant a small amount of the reinforcer in order to encourage the desired behavior
    c. mixing extinction and positive reinforcement
    d. mixing positive and negative reinforcement
    e. testing the various reinforcers available to determine which one should be applied

Now that you have completed the evaluation, please check your answers with those listed in the back of the book. When you are satisfied with the degree to which you have retained the information, please turn the page to begin work on the next chapter.

15 CHAIN BEHAVIORS TOGETHER

Chaining is another behavior analysis procedure that can be used to teach new behaviors to program participants. A *chain* is a sequence of steps that must be completed to correctly perform a terminal behavior. Each correctly completed step serves as a stimulus for the initiation of the next step in the sequence. When the final step of the series is completed, the program participant is positively reinforced. The sequence of steps related to the performance of a terminal behavior is sometimes referred to as a *behavioral chain*. The process of identifying a series of steps and guiding the program participant through these steps over a period of training sessions is know as *chaining*.

A procedure that facilitates the chaining process is called task analysis. *Task analysis* involves the precise delineation and sequencing of the components of an identified task or objective to facilitate individualized learning. By conducting a task analysis, the leisure service professional can systematically determine an instructional sequence of identified content that has been divided into manageable amounts of information.

Task analysis allows the service provider to identify the content that can be taught through the chaining procedure. Through task analysis followed by the chaining procedure, the participant can learn an entire skill by initially learning segments of the skill, thus facilitating the acquisition of new material with a maximum amount of success.

Task analysis is conducted by examining the terminal behavior and considering the skills and abilities of the individual participant. Therefore, the leisure service professional must continually examine the individual's progress when teaching the skill through chaining. If an individual is encountering difficulty progressing to the next task, it may be due to the fact that the task analysis was not complete. The current task analysis should be examined to determine if enough subtasks have been identified to completely cover the performance of the main task and identify any essential subtasks that have been omitted.

> As an example, perhaps Shang-Ti has not been allowed to move fast enough through the learning process associated with playing golf and has begun to get bored with learning this task. Coral may have delineated too many subtasks associated with swinging a golf club, included tasks that are not actually necessary to complete the terminal behavior, or repeated a subtask. Therefore, Coral examines the task analysis to determine if any subtasks are trivial, unnecessary, or redundant.

The following is an example of a task analysis for baking cookies.

1. Locate the oven.
2. Preheat the oven to 425 degrees.
3. Locate a recipe card.
4. Place all dry ingredients in one bowl.
5. Mix ingredients.

6. In a separate bowl, place eggs and liquid ingredients.

7. Mix together liquid ingredients and dry ingredients.

8. Spray a cookie sheet with non-stick oil.

9. Drop one tablespoon of cookie dough on cookie sheet.

10. Repeat this step two inches next to the previous drop.

11. Continue dropping cookie dough on cookie sheet until approximately 12 cookies are dropped.

12. Place cookie sheet in the oven.

13. Set timer for 8-10 minutes.

14. Check the cookies for brownness.

15. Remove cookies from oven when cooked.

16. Let cookies cool until ready to eat.

Now that you have seen an example of a task analysis, try the following exercise. You would like to teach Silvia how to bowl. To explain this task, you have decided to conduct a task analysis by segmenting into 10 steps the skill of moving to the release line and throwing the ball. List the ten steps you have identified in the spaces provided.

1. _____

2. _____

3. _____

4. _____

5. _____

6. _____

7. _____

8. _____

9. _____

10. _____

If your steps resemble those presented below, it appears you are catching on.

1. Picks up bowling ball with both hands.

2. Puts fingers of dominant hand in holes.

3. Grips ball in dominant hand with the other hand under the ball.

4. Holds ball in front of body while standing three steps from the release line with feet together.

5. Points thumb of dominant hand toward pins, thumb up, wrist straight.

6. Holds ball forward with dominant hand and steps forward with dominant foot.

7. Lowers ball to side of leg and close to body and steps forward with other foot.

8. Draws ball back past body while bending knees and steps forward with dominant foot.

9. Brings ball forward while continuing to bend knees and steps forward with other foot just in front of the release line.

10. Releases ball in front of other foot six inches from the floor.

When chaining a terminal behavior, each step in the chain has a consequence that serves as a conditioned reinforcer for that particular step and also as an antecedent to the next step in the series. A *conditioned reinforcer* is any stimulus that was not previously a reinforcer but has acquired the properties of such by association with a stimulus that is a reinforcer. All steps in the sequence have this characteristic, except the final step. The final step in the chain is followed by the completion of the task.

Task completion results in enhanced participation. Participation in many leisure pursuits is usually enjoyable and provides the necessary reinforcement for task completion.

> For example, Akbar may decide to use chaining to teach Leona to kick a ball to prepare her to play soccer. The initial phase of the chaining procedure is to identify the sequence of steps that must be correctly completed Leona to perform the behavior of "kicking a ball."
>
> The action of kicking a ball can be separated into the following sequence of steps:
>
> - stand with weight evenly distributed on both feet
> - shift weight to right foot
> - step forward with left foot
> - shift weight to left foot
> - swing right leg forward
> - contact ball with toes of right foot
>
> The opportunity to kick the soccer ball would serve as the stimulus for Leona to perform the first step in the sequence; that is, standing with her weight evenly distributed on both feet. Performance of this first step will serve as a stimulus for performing the second step. Completion of the second step in the sequence, shifting the weight to the right foot, reinforces the first step and acts as a stimulus for performing the third step. This process continues through all the steps in the chain until the final step is performed. Performance of the final step is reinforced when Leona has successfully kicked the soccer ball.

The previous example demonstrates the process of forward chaining. *Forward chaining* involves teaching the sequence of steps in the order in which they will normally occur. The first step in the chain is taught first, followed by the second step and so on. Depending on the behavior to be learned and the participant who is to learn it, forward chaining can be an appropriate procedure to utilize.

A common way to teach a behavior that has been separated into a sequence of steps is called backward chaining. ***Backward chaining*** involves teaching the steps in the reverse order that they normally will occur in the chain. The last step in the chain will be taught first. When this step is performed at an appropriate level, the participant is then taught the next to last step in the chain. When the next to last step is performed correctly, the participant is presented with the opportunity to perform the last step (which has already been mastered). Completion of the last step of a recreation activity will typically result in an enjoyable experience and thus be considered to be a positive reinforcement.

> In the example of Leona being taught to kick the soccer ball, backward chaining would be an appropriate procedure to employ. The final step in the sequence of steps was identified as "swinging the right leg forward, contacting the ball with the toes of the right foot." This is the step that is taught first. It could be taught by Akbar by placing the ball directly in front of the Leona's right foot and prompting her to kick the ball. The correct performance of this final step would be followed by positive reinforcement. In this case, the positive reinforcement is the enjoyment experienced by Leona by propelling the ball. When Leona has demonstrated that she can consistently perform the final step, she would then be taught the next to last step.
>
> The next to last step in this sequence was identified as "swinging the right leg backward." Akbar teaches this step by placing the soccer ball several inches away from the Leona's right foot and again instructing her to kick the ball. Leona then has to swing her right leg backward (the next to last step) to swing it forward and make contact with the ball (the final step). Performance of the final step again provides positive reinforcement. This procedure is followed back through the steps of the chain. The final task for the Leona to complete would be learning the first step in the sequence. When Leona has successfully mastered all of the steps in the chain, she will have developed the fundamental skill of kicking a soccer ball. She will have learned a terminal behavior and be ready to learn other new behaviors that will enable her to experience enjoyment from participating in a soccer game.

There are two major advantages associated with backward chaining that are not present with forward chaining. First, backward chaining guarantees that when teaching begins for any step in the chain the consequence of the step will always be reinforced. Second, backward chaining avoids disruption of a previously established sequence of steps and consequences. Once a consequence has been arranged to follow a given step, it will always continue to follow the same step. This prevents the step from stopping due to extinction.

Advantages of backward chaining include the following:

- **The consequence of the steps will always be reinforced.**
- Avoids disruption of previously established steps.

Although chaining and shaping are both procedures used to teach new behaviors, there are substantial differences between the two. In **shaping**, the successive approximations are discarded (through extinction) as progress is made toward the terminal behavior. When the terminal behavior is established, the successive approximations are no longer needed. In **chaining**, all of the steps are essential in order to perform the terminal behavior correctly and thus they are all retained. In shaping, the learning proceeds in a forward mode; the sequence of tasks is from first to last. In chaining, the process is most often reversed.

Shaping is the appropriate procedure to employ when the new behavior to be learned is a refinement of an approximation or a modification of a form of a behavior. Shaping can be done in a more loosely structured environment because approximations of the behavior are acceptable; correct performance of a step in a series of steps is not required in shaping as it is in chaining. Chaining can be employed when the behavior to be learned is capable of being separated in a series of discrete steps. Chaining requires a more structured environment because the steps must be performed correctly; approximations of the step generally are not adequate for mastery of the behavior.

Please turn to the next page and evaluate how well you retained the information presented on chaining.

Test Your Knowledge of Chaining

1. Brenda performs the individual steps needed for her to go to a movie; however, she does not complete them in the correct sequence. After identifying six steps involved in going to a movie, you decide to teach her these skills. You choose to teach Brenda by having her perform step 1 and then assist her with steps 2–6. Once she has learned this step, you require her to perform steps 1 and 2. You then assist her with steps 3–6. What teaching procedure have you implemented if you continue in this manner?

    a. alternate shaping
    b. backward chaining
    c. forward chaining
    d. graduated guidance
    e. longitudinal cuing

2. Damion learned to ride public transportation, read at the library, and check out a book. What is the next step in teaching Damion to use the community library?

    a. accelerate the three skills
    b. chain the three skills
    c. fade the three skills
    d. reinforce the three skills
    e. shape the three skills

Based on the next paragraph, please answer the two associated questions.

Calvin was in a woodworking session. To complete his project, he had to pick up a board, lay it in a jig, drill a hole in it, insert a dowel, and then give it to the leader. A problem arose one day when the drill bit was dull and would not make the hole in the wood. Calvin picked up a board, laid it in the jig, attempted to drill a hole, and then stopped. After stopping he simply sat at his work area and looked around the room.

3. What was the reinforcement that usually followed the entire behavioral chain?

    a. drilling the hole
    b. giving the project to the leader
    c. inserting the dowel
    d. laying the board in the jig
    e. picking up the board

4. What was the antecedent condition that did not occur in order for Calvin to complete the chain?

    a. drilling the hole
    b. giving the project to the leader
    c. inserting the dowel
    d. laying the board in the jig
    e. picking up the board

5. What is the purpose of chaining?

    a. allow program participants an opportunity to associate leisure with learning
    b. develop a new behavior
    c. extinguish inappropriate behavior
    d. link conditioned reinforcement with inappropriate behaviors
    e. link extinction with positive reinforcement

6. A chain may be defined as a series of steps that must be accomplished to do what?

    a. connect extinction with positive reinforcement
    b. ensure that each behavior has an antecedent and a consequence
    c. ensure that leisure experiences are educational
    d. successfully perform a terminal behavior
    e. weaken an inappropriate behavior

7. What does the chaining procedure involve?

    a. associating leisure education with recreation activities
    b. following a sequence of steps to weaken an inappropriate behavior
    c. linking together several separate behavior modification procedures
    d. the identification of a sequence of steps and guidance of a participant through those steps to mastery of a new behavior
    e. the identification of a series of steps aimed at improving general fitness

8. What is a series of steps that must be correctly performed to master a new behavior referred to as?

    a. a behavioral chain
    b. a behavioral stimulus
    c. a terminal behavior
    d. conditioned reinforcers
    e. conditioned stimuli

9. What is a conditioned reinforcer?

    a. behavior that reinforces itself
    b. physical exercise aimed at improving general fitness
    c. reinforcer that can only be applied according to predetermined conditions
    d. stimulus that has acquired reinforcing properties through association with a reinforcer
    e. stimulus that intermittently has reinforcing properties

10. What is backward chaining?

    a. a procedure that, because of its undesirable side effects, should be used only if other methods have been tried and failed
    b. a procedure that involves teaching the steps in a behavioral chain in reverse order to their normal occurrence
    c. first applying positive reinforcement and then applying extinction
    d. sequential steps taken to eliminate a previously learned behavior
    e. the phase applied to the procedure when the participant is extremely slow in learning the required steps

11. What is forward chaining?

    a. a procedure that first applies negative reinforcement and then applies extinction
    b. a procedure that involves teaching a sequence of steps for a behavior in the order in which they would normally appear
    c. a sequence of steps taken to punish an inappropriate behavior
    d. stimulation of aggression and other undesirable traits in participants
    e. the phrase used when the participant is exceptionally quick in mastering the steps required for a new behavior

12. How are chaining and shaping similar? They both:

    a. are designed to teach new behaviors.
    b. improve a participant's general fitness level.
    c. rely on extinction of previously learned behaviors.
    d. rely on successive approximations of behavior.
    e. utilize extinction.

13. In the chaining procedure, the stimulus for the initiation of a step in the sequence is provided by:

    a. correct completion of the preceding step.
    b. extinction.
    c. negative reinforcement.
    d. punishment.
    e. shaping.

14. In the chaining procedure, positive reinforcement is provided to the individual:

    a. after the completion of the first step.
    b. at the discretion of the training staff.
    c. only if the individual is unable to complete the task.
    d. when the final step of the series is completed.
    e. whenever the individual requests it.

15. A major advantage associated with backward chaining is that:

    a. extinction can be substituted for positive reinforcement.
    b. punishment can be easily applied as a learning stimulus.
    c. the consequence of any step in the chain is always reinforced.
    d. the steps are taught in the sequence in which they naturally occur.
    e. the steps can be taught in any sequence.

Now that you have completed the evaluation, please check your answers with the ones listed in the back of the book. If needed, review the material and try the exercises again.

16 PROVIDE DISCRETE TRIALS

Discrete trials are used to teach specific concepts or skills through the use of repetition and positive reinforcement. A *trial* is an opportunity for a person to make a correct or incorrect response. In this instance, the word *discrete* is used to describe a trial that has a specific beginning and ending point. The specific beginning is the stimulus and the specific ending is the response. The process of using discrete trials is sometimes called the use of *mass trials* because of the repetition involved in the presentation of directions and rewards. Often, a concept is presented in sets of 10 trials. The first step in using a discrete trial is to **identify** the concept or skill to be taught.

> For example, a discrete trial designed to increase Dierdre's knowledge could involve teaching Dierdre to identify equipment used to play tennis. A skill discrete trial could include shooting a foul shot using a basketball.

The second step in implementing a discrete trial is to **present** a direction. A sample direction might be "Show me a tennis ball." or "Shoot a free throw." The third step of a discrete trial is to **prompt** the behavior. For instance, the following sentence could be stated: "Show me a tennis ball." while pointing to a tennis ball. Or "Shoot a free throw, like this." while demonstrating the action. The final step is to **reward** the target behavior by saying something such as the following: "It is nice that you showed me the tennis ball, you can now hit the ball with a tennis racquet." or "The arc on the basketball was just right!"

To review, when using discrete trials to teach a leisure skills it is helpful to complete the following steps:

1. **Identify** the concept or skill
2. **Present** a direction
3. **Prompt** the target behavior
4. **Reward** the target behavior

It is important that the concept or skill being taught be relatively simple, such as completing one step in a sequence of tasks.

> For example, when teaching Mustafa to color, the act of putting the crayon on paper would be the target behavior. Selecting a crayon and coloring within the lines would be additional skills that are taught at a later time.

The target behavior should be easy for everyone to **identify**. Such a target behavior for Hailey could be for her to turn on an electronic device. This technique can be used to teach participants a variety of skills needed to engage in recreation activities. Once the participant and service provider work collaboratively to identify a skill or concept to be taught, it is time for the directions to be **presented**. Some examples of directions include:

- "Touch tennis" to identify a picture of someone playing tennis.
- "Let's walk" to go for a walk.
- "Play video game" to play a video game.
- "Paint" to hold a paint brush.

If the participant does not perform a task independently, **prompts** will likely need to be used.

> For example, to play a drum, the leisure service provider, Marja, provides the following directions: "play drum." If Lan "plays the drum" she will be given a reward such as attention from a desired person. If Lan does not play the drum given verbal directions, a *visual prompt* used in conjunction with the *verbal prompt* can be provided, such as: "play the drum like me" accompanied by a demonstration of how to play the drum. If Lan still does not play the drum, a *physical prompt* can be paired with the verbal prompt. For example, Marja can gently take Lan's hand to help Lan play the drum.

This sequence of prompting is often called "3-Step Prompting" and is summarized by the steps:

1. **Tell**: using a verbal prompt
2. **Show**: using a visual prompt
3. **Do**: using a physical prompt

Often, it is valuable for the participant to attempt or complete the task independently; in this case a *prompt delay* might be implemented. A ***prompt delay*** is the period of time that transpires between when the desired behavior can occur and when the prompt is presented. A 5-second time delay may be used.

> For example, Phoebe is directed to "paint a picture." Omar, the leisure service provider, then silently counts to 5. After five seconds have elapsed, Omar says: "Phoebe, please paint a picture like me." while demonstrating the act of painting. Omar then silently counts to 5. Once five seconds have elapsed, Omar physically guides Phoebe through the action of painting. As Omar helps Phoebe paint the picture, he says: "You are painting a picture."

The final step of discrete trials is to **reward** an individual for correct responses. Positive reinforcement typically is used if a person independently completes the task either before or after the verbal direction. If shaping or chaining (concepts outlined in other chapters) are used, the reinforcement might occur after the visual prompt.

> For instance, if Jenji, the leisure service provider, asks Martin to "throw the ball" and Martin is nonresponsive, meaning he sits and does not make movements associated with throwing a ball after several trials; Jenji then says: "Throw the ball, like me." while demonstrating how to throw the ball. If Martin throws the ball, Jenji praises Martin each time he throws the ball saying "Nice throw Marty!" or a variation of that phrase.

If reinforcement is used after each step, the most preferred reinforcement (the item identified during the preference assessment as being chosen the most) is provided after the verbal directions. The least preferred reinforcement (the item identified during the preference assessment as a reward but was not the favorite item) occurs after the physical prompt.

When using discrete trials, the initial set of trials involves the application of continuous reinforcement. As a reminder, ***continuous reinforcement*** involves reinforcement administered after demonstration of each successful behavior. ***Intermittent reinforcement***, reinforcement that is administered occasionally—*not* after every time the target behavior occurs, is used to maintain acquired knowledge and mastered skills.

> As an illustration, Hope learned to color during a discrete trial session. When learning to color, Bart provided Hope with a sticker for her sticker book each time she completed the task. After she mastered the act of coloring, Bart enrolled Hope in an art class. Now Bart gives Hope a sticker after she paints a complete picture.

Again, to summarize, the process of using discrete trials involves:

1. **Identify** the concepts and skills to be taught.
2. **Present** a direction to introduce the concept or skill.
3. **Prompt** a correct response if necessary.
4. **Reward** all correct responses.

As an illustration, if José is taught to identify recreation activities during a session, this session might look like the following exchange between the service provider and José:

1. Present a picture of a tennis racket and ball.
2. Say "Touch tennis."
3. José does not respond.
4. Count silently to five and then say: "Touch tennis, like me," while touching the tennis picture.
5. José continues to not respond to the prompt.
6. Count silently to five then help José touch the tennis picture.
7. Say: "This is touching tennis."

These seven steps equate to a trial. The second trial might resemble the following.

1. Present a picture of a tennis racket and ball.
2. Say: "Touch tennis."
3. José does nothing.
4. Count silently to five and then say: "Touch tennis, like me." while touching the tennis picture.
5. José touches the tennis picture.
6. Say: "You did terrific touching tennis."

After completing these steps, continue immediately to a third trial that might proceed as follows.

1. Present a picture of a tennis racket and ball.
2. Say: "Touch tennis."
3. José touches the picture of tennis.
4. Say: "Nice work touching tennis." and give José reinforcement.

It is helpful when providing such instructions to continue these trials until José is provided with directions 10 times in one sitting, this is also called a set. The criterion of 80% successful completions can be established. A *criterion* is a standard that is set to identify that a skill has been successfully demonstrated. Therefore, it is stipulated that José needs to demonstrate 80% independent card touches (8 of the 10 opportunities) before a new recreation activity such as basketball, swimming, or bowling is introduced. When the new activity is introduced it is presented in the same manner.

1. Present a picture of a basketball.
2. Say: "Touch basketball."

3. José does nothing.

4. Count silently to five, then say: "Touch basketball, like me," while touching the picture of a basketball.

5. José still does nothing.

6. Count silently to five, then physically help José touch the picture of a basketball.

7. Say: "That is touching basketball."

These seven steps equate to a trial. The second trial might occur as follows:

1. Present a picture of a basketball.

2. Say: "Touch basketball."

3. José does nothing.

4. Count to five silently, then say: "Touch basketball, like me."

5. José touches the picture of a basketball.

6. Say: "Well done touching basketball, José," and provide reinforcement.

Instruction continues immediately to a third trial that might resemble the following:

1. Present a picture of a basketball.

2. Say: "Touch basketball."

3. José touches the picture of basketball.

4. Say: "Now you are touching basketball!" and provide José with reinforcement.

José's responses can be entered onto a recording sheet. It is helpful if a recording sheet for a discrete trial contains the trial number, correct and incorrect responses, the types of prompts used, and the length of the prompt delay. A recording sheet may be established as follows:

When Jose' successfully completes the steps to identify tennis balls and basketballs, both cards are presented simultaneously to determine if he discriminates between these two concepts. Discrimination training is discussed in Chapter 19.

Trial #	Correct (+) or Incorrect (-)	Visual Prompt	Physical Prompt	Prompt Delay
1				
2				
3				
4				
5				
6				
7				
8				
9				
10				

1. Now it is your turn. Identify a skill that you would like to teach an individual.

   _____

2. What specific instruction will you give this individual during each trial?

   _____

3. What specific response are you looking for the individual to demonstrate?

   _____

4. What do you do if the individual does not respond with 5 seconds?

   _____

5. What do you do if the individual still does not respond?

   _____

Reflect on the responses to the previous questions.

- Was the activity simple?
- Was the instruction concise?
- Were the responses observable and measurable?
- Did you use visual prompting and physical prompting when necessary?

In this chapter we discussed using discrete trials to teach specific concepts or skills through the use of repetition and positive reinforcement. When using discrete trials we follow the following steps:

- **Identify** the concepts and skills to be taught.
- **Present** a direction to introduce the concept or skill.
- **Prompt** a correct response if necessary.
- **Reward** all correct responses.

You have now completed the information on providing discrete trials. Please go to the next page and evaluate how well you retained the material.

Test Your Knowledge of Providing Discrete Trials

1. The term used to describe an opportunity for a person to make a correct or incorrect response is known as:

    a. antecedent.
    b. discrimination.
    c. discrete.
    d. mass.
    e. trial.

2. The term used to describe repetitive presentation of a stimulus or response is called:

    a. antecedent.
    b. discrimination.
    c. discrete.
    d. mass.
    e. trial.

3. This term is used to denote a specific beginning and ending:

    a. antecedent.
    b. discrimination.
    c. discrete.
    d. mass.
    e. trial.

4. The following method of prompting is used first when teaching a new skill or concept:

    a. correctional (redo)
    b. physical (do)
    c. positional (try)
    d. verbal (say)
    e. visual (show)

5. This method of prompting involves demonstration of a skill:

    a. correctional (redo)
    b. physical (do)
    c. positional (try)
    d. verbal (say)
    e. visual (show)

6. The method of prompting that involves using hand over hand guidance is:

    a. correctional (redo)
    b. physical (do)
    c. positional (try)
    d. verbal (say)
    e. visual (show)

7. Instructions in discrete trials are called:

   a. discriminative stimulus.
   b. discriminative response.
   c. discrete stimulus.
   d. discrete response.
   e. mass stimulus.

8. Instructions in discrete trials should be:

   a. abstract.
   b. concrete.
   c. challenging.
   d. difficult.
   e. easy.

9. The period of time that transpires between when the desired behavior can occur and when a prompt is delivered is called:

   a. prompt delay.
   b. reinforcement delay.
   c. response lag.
   d. time delay
   e. stimulus lag.

10. The target behavior in a discrete trial is the:

   a. antecedent.
   b. prompt.
   c. response.
   d. stimulus.
   e. reinforcement.

11. A standard that denotes that a skill has been successfully demonstrated is called:

   a. assessment.
   b. baseline.
   c. behavior.
   d. condition.
   e. criterion.

12. Saying "Touch baseball" is an example of the following type of prompt:

   a. environmental
   b. physical
   c. positional
   d. verbal
   e. visual

13. Saying "Nice going, touching baseball" is an example of:

    a. instruction.
    b. prompt.
    c. response.
    d. reward.
    e. none of the above.

14. If a participant does not respond to a visual prompt, the following occurs:

    a. Change the expectation.
    b. Repeat the visual prompt.
    c. Provide a physical prompt.
    d. Use a verbal prompt.
    e. Wait five seconds and provide a verbal prompt.

15. The following item from the preference assessment is used as reinforcement for a participant who complies with a new instruction without any prompting:

    a. a standard reinforcement
    b. a moderately preferred item
    c. a novel item
    d. the highest preferred item
    e. the least preferred item

Now that you have completed the evaluation, please check your answers with the ones listed in the back of the book. When you are satisfied with your retention of the information, you are ready to begin work on the next chapter.

17 DEVELOP FUNCTIONAL COMMUNICATION

Behavior analysis procedures that can be used to encourage individuals to communicate are the focus of this chapter. Once a functional assessment is conducted to identify potential causes of a behavior such as seeking attention, obtaining a desired item or activity, or escaping from undesirable situations or demands, an important step is to teach effective ways to communicate.

The ability to successfully communicate creates the opportunity for individuals to obtain someone's attention, a desired item, or an interesting activity. Also, effective communication allows people to determine ways to remove themselves from an undesirable situation without engaging in behaviors that may disrupt the enjoyment or learning of others and themselves or cause harm to others or themselves.

As identified in previous chapters, there are many ways to teach a new skill using positive reinforcement that can be used to facilitate leisure engagement. Since so much of leisure participation involves social interaction, teaching people effective ways to communicate should help them to engage in meaningful and enjoyable leisure. Consequently, the purpose of this chapter is to present information about teaching a person how to communicate within a leisure context.

Collaborate with Speech Language Pathologists

Before details about how to teach communication skills are presented, the concept of communication is described. Two concepts often associated with communication are linguistics and phonetics. *Linguistics* is the study of language, such as how and why certain words are used, whereas *phonetics* is the study of speech involving how sounds are made. Speech language pathologists are trained in these areas and can be useful resources when helping individuals develop communication skills.

If communication within a leisure context is one of the goals for a person, it is important that consultation occurs with a speech language pathologist. If an individual has encountered difficulty with speech or language, a speech language pathologist may have developed a communication system for that individual. A speech language pathologist might work on articulation by shaping sounds or may have established a communication system such as a communication book or using an electronic tablet as a communication system. It may be helpful if leisure service professionals work with a speech language pathologist to include leisure concepts in the person's communication system. Leisure service professionals might also work within the leisure context to reinforce communication skills being taught by speech language pathologists.

Types of Communication and Associated Instructional Strategies

Communication is the process of conveying a message between two or more people. The person who wants to initiate a message is often called a sender and the person who interprets the message is called the receiver. *Receptive communication* involves receiving the message and *expressive communication* is the process associated with sending the message. Expressive communication can occur verbally, using visual aids, or gestures. Such expressive communication can be as simple as pointing to a desired item or as complex as using various methods of sign language.

Receptive communication. An important aspect of learning to communicate is developing receptive communication skills. This process usually begins with **discrete trials.** *Discrete trials* involve the repetition of several trials that have a specific stimulus and response (the use of discrete trails is described in further detail in subsequent chapters). The service provider repeats a prompt to encourage a person to respond correctly on multiple, consecutive occasions.

For example, Hsian is presented with a tube of paint and a paintbrush. He is then taught to touch the paintbrush after a specific prompt. The prompt is the actual presentation of the paintbrush, or it might include the statement, "Touch the paintbrush." This type of prompt is often called the discriminative stimulus because Hsian is learning to discriminate or learn the difference between words such as "tube of paint" and "paintbrush." Once one concept has been mastered, Hsian is then provided with two additional items, such as a pallet and a canvas, one at a time until he masters the skill of touching an object or picture when prompted to do so. Each time he touches the object or picture, the concepts associated with the object or picture become the focus of the instruction. New topics associated with goals of the leisure program can be gradually introduced to increase Hsian's leisure repertoire.

Expressive communication. Once a participant's receptive language repertoire is identified, then the person can be supported to develop functional verbal skills. Verbal behavior can be conveyed in a variety of ways from echoing what another person says to assigning meaning and feelings to activities. Two common verbal behaviors are called **mands** and **tacts**. *Mands* are when a person makes a request for an activity or item.

An example of a mand is if Phoebe says, "I would like to go outside, please." San Pedro then responds to Phoebe in a variety of ways depending on the circumstances. One response is to accompany her outside to the patio. When possible, it is helpful to respond to and teach mands that help participants obtain access to a desired activity.

Tacts are when a person describes an item or activity.

An example of a tact is if Omar says, "I enjoy playing soccer." Elaina then responds by encouraging Omar to describe his preferences and assign meaning to recreation activities by making such statements as: "When did you last play soccer?" or "What is your favorite part about playing soccer?"

The two examples with Phoebe and Omar involve the use of complex sentences and some individuals might have difficulty making statements like these. At times it may be appropriate to begin with simple words.

As an example, Jillian may begin mastering one word at a time such as "ball," then move to two-word statements such as "red ball." When Jillian masters two words, she might learn four-word statements, such as, "I want red ball," then progress to six-word phrases such as, "Belinda, I want the red ball." This would be an example of how chaining is used to teach communication.

When teaching expressive communication, it is helpful to identify a person's current communication skills. Answers to the following questions are important:

- Can the person speak?
- How many words does the person say?
- What sounds can the person make?

If the participant is capable of speaking and making sounds, then it is helpful if the person uses words that are respectful and not offensive to others to make requests.

> As an example, if Arianna wants to spend some time alone, it is beneficial to teach her that saying, "Leave me the [explicative] alone" is not acceptable; rather, a verbal statement such as saying, "Please allow me to be alone for a few minutes" will more likely lead to positive results. In another example, if Cristiano does not speak clearly but uses sounds, sounds such as "dah, dah, dah," these can be shaped into words such as "doll."

Shaping is often the technique used to help teach a person to verbalize an entire word when the individual currently only vocalizes a portion of a word.

> For instance, shaping the word ball from "bah" starts with the use of continuous reinforcement for the "bah" sound. Therefore, every time that Nolan says "bah," he receives a ball. Once he masters saying "bah" when he wants the ball, Sarah, the leisure service professional, says, "ball." Nolan then might say "bail" and continuous reinforcement will be used every time Nolan says a word that begins with "b" and ends with "l." Once Nolan consistently uses the word "bail" for "ball," Sarah uses intermittent reinforcement. Sarah then says, "ball," and Nolan says, "ball."

Verbal communication might not be possible with some people. This is when **augmentative and alternative communication (AAC)** methods and devices can be used. *Augmentative* communication systems supplement a person's existing method of communication, such as writing when speech is not clear, while *alternative* communication systems allow for speech to occur through another medium such as a computerized system of speech. Devices for communication range from a pictorial communication symbol board to electronic devices such as computers with voice output and extensive memory programmed to meet the needs of each individual. AAC systems and devices are designed to empower individuals to independently communicate, make choices, and express preferences, which are all important for leisure engagement.

If an individual has writing or typing skills, the person might use paper and a writing instrument or an electronic tablet to facilitate communication. Similar to the example of shaping verbal behavior, the words being written can be shaped from those that are not effectively facilitating communication to those that promote communication.

If the individual has neither verbal nor written communication skills, the person may use a picture or object exchange system. A *picture or object communication exchange system* involves an individual pointing to a picture or object to express a need or desire. Sometimes individuals may hand a picture or object to a leisure service professional who can assist them in meeting their needs.

It is useful to be aware of the communication systems used at home, school, or work so that there is consistency when communicating within a leisure context. Introducing new words, concepts, and activities into a person's existing communication system helps to expand the participant's expressive language repertoire.

In summary, communication is a process by which individuals express themselves using words, gestures, or pictures. Principles of applied behavior analysis such as positive reinforcement, shaping, and discrete trials can be used to expand a person's expressive and receptive language repertoire. To teach these skills, the leisure service professional:

- **Assesses** the communication skills and needs of an individual.
- **Uses** existing communication systems if available.
- **Teaches** new language skills if appropriate.

Now that we have addressed some ways to teach communication skills, try to answer the following questions:

1. If Latoya says, "Bah, goo, la, and ti," what are some leisure words you could try to teach her to say?

_____

_____

_____

2. What type of pictures and words would you include on a communication device for Jeremiah who attends a day camp?

_____

_____

_____

3. What types of pictures and words would you include on a communication device for Cleo who comes to your fitness facilities?

_____

_____

_____

- In the first example, did you select words for Latoya that begin with the letters "b, g, t, and l"? Did these words include the vowel sounds of "ah" "oo" and "ee?"
- In the second example, did you identify leisure pursuits for Jeremiah, or did you list activities of daily living such as going to the bathroom, eating, or drinking?
- For Cleo in the third example, did you include fitness equipment or body parts?

In this chapter, ways that functional communication can be used in leisure contexts are described. Expressive communication involves the process of sending a message. Receptive communication involves how an individual receives the message. In leisure contexts, professionals might need to do the following:

1. **Assess** the communication skills and needs of an individual.
2. **Use** existing communication systems if available.
3. **Teach** new language skills if appropriate.

Please go to the next page and evaluate how well you retained the information presented on functional communication.

Test Your Knowledge of Developing Functional Communication

1. What is the process of conveying a message between two or more people called?

    a. behavior analysis
    b. communication
    c. discrimination
    d. expression
    e. listening

2. A form of communication that involves understanding a message that was sent to a receiver is called:

    a. alternative.
    b. augmentative.
    c. expressive.
    d. receptive.
    e. repetitive.

3. This form of communication involves sending another person information about one's needs, interests, wants, and desires:

    a. alternative
    b. augmentative
    c. expressive
    d. receptive
    e. repetitive

4. Which of the following techniques is often used as an initial strategy to teach receptive communication?

    a. chaining
    b. discrete trials
    c. shaping
    d. response restriction
    e. tact training

5. This statement is used at the beginning of a discrete trial:

    a. discrete instruction
    b. discrete response
    c. discriminative stimulus
    d. discriminative response
    e. response restriction

6. Which form of expressive communication involves making a request?

    a. discrimination
    b. phonetics
    c. linguistics
    d. mands
    e. tacts

7. Which form of expressive communication describes an item or activity?

    a. discrimination
    b. phonetics
    c. linguistics
    d. mands
    e. tacts

8. Grant lost his ability to vocalize words so he tells people what he wants by writing in a notebook. This type of communication is called:

    a. ancillary.
    b. assistive.
    c. alternative.
    d. augmentative.
    e. discriminative.

9. Sydney uses a program on her electronic device that speaks what she types. This is an example of which type of communication?

    a. ancillary
    b. assistive
    c. alternative
    d. augmentative
    e. discriminative

10. Paola makes the "puh" sound. The technique that is often used to teach Paola how to say the word puzzle is called what?

    a. chaining
    b. discrete trials
    c. shaping
    d. response restriction
    e. tact training

11. Nat is in a social skills group where Lev is teaching him to say, "I want the ball, please," instead of merely saying the word "ball." What is the technique that is likely being used with Nat called?

    a. chaining
    b. discrete trials
    c. shaping
    d. response restriction
    e. tact training

12. Ronaldo uses an electronic tablet device for recreation and speaks clearly using one-word phrases. What is the technique that is often used to teach him to communicate called?

    a. chaining
    b. discrete trials
    c. shaping
    d. response restriction
    e. tact training

13. Saying "I like to play ping pong" is an example of

    a. discrimination.
    b. phonetics.
    c. linguistics.
    d. mands.
    e. tacts.

14. Juan learned to identify the names of songs by using a repetitive series of commands and responses. This is an example of:

    a. chaining.
    b. discrete trials.
    c. shaping.
    d. response restriction.
    e. tact training.

15. The statement "I want to swim, please" is an example of:

    a. discrimination.
    b. phonetics.
    c. linguistics.
    d. mands.
    e. tacts.

After completing the evaluation, please check your answers with those recorded in the back of the book. When you are satisfied with the knowledge you have acquired, please turn the page and begin work on the next chapter.

18 PROMOTE DISCRIMINATION

Once a participant understands a few concepts or develops some skills, it is valuable to help the person determine when and in what situations it would be useful to apply knowledge or demonstrate various skills. It is often helpful to assist participants in differentiating between behaviors that typically result in positive responses and those that tend to result in undesirable responses. When behaviors result in positive responses, the individual is more likely to be successful and experience leisure. The process of helping a person make these distinctions between situations is called ***discrimination.***

Some functions of discrimination are as follows:

- To **expand** an individual's knowledge or skill base.
- To **assess** an individual's understanding of concepts.
- To **control** situations.

When using discrimination to **expand** or assess a participant's understanding of skills or concepts, discrimination training can be used in conjunction with discrete trials to expand a person's knowledge or increase their skills.

> For example, if Josephine wants to learn about sports, she can work with Corliss to differentiate between 10 different sports by learning to distinguish between pictures that present the 10 sports. Therefore, Corliss would first teach Josephine to identify a tennis picture when Corliss states: "Tennis." through the discrete trial process. Once Josephine masters pointing to the tennis picture and, subsequently, masters pointing to the basketball picture through the discrete trial process, Corliss works with her to discriminate between the two topics. There are three ways that Corliss could do this:

- Random rotation
- Expanded trials
- Positional prompts

Random rotation is a process that involves the presentation of two different items by asking the participant to identify two items that the person has successfully identified on previous occasions.

A session using random rotation might involve the following:

Trial 1: Corliss says, "Touch tennis," and Josephine touches the tennis card.

Trial 2: Corliss says, "Touch basketball," and Josephine touches the basketball card.

Trial 3: Corliss says, "Touch tennis," and Josephine touches the tennis card.

Trial 4: Corliss says, "Touch tennis," and Josephine touches the tennis card.

Trial 5: Corliss says, "Touch basketball," and Josephine touches the basketball card.

Trial 6: Corliss says, "Touch basketball," and Josephine touches the basketball card.

Trial 7: Corliss says, "Touch tennis," and Josephine touches the tennis card.

Trial 8: Corliss says, "Touch basketball," and Josephine touches the basketball card.

Trial 9: Corliss says, "Touch basketball," and Josephine touches the basketball card.

Trial 10: Corliss says, "Touch tennis," and Josephine touches the tennis card.

Behavior Analysis in Leisure Contexts

Presentation of the cards is alternated between presenting the card on the left side or right side. In addition, the order of the verbal presentation of the cards is alternated.

> Once Josephine masters these two concepts by providing correct responses associated with an established criterion, such as 8 out of the 10 trials, new concepts such as "baseball" and "soccer" can be introduced in the same manner.
> When Josephine successfully identifies 10 recreation activities, including such activities as tennis, basketball, walking, soccer, golf, swimming, sailing, surfing, skiing, horseback riding, and bowling, new activities can be introduced using a process called expanded trials.

The process of *expanded trials* involves providing an additional concept by implementing mass trials. When using expanded trials, a new activity is introduced.

> For example, when working with Josephine an 11th recreation activity is introduced such as "hiking." Initially, hiking is introduced using mass trials of the new concept as illustrated in the following:

Trial 1: Corliss says, "Touch hiking." Josephine touches the hiking card.

Trial 2: Corliss says, "Touch hiking." Josephine touches the hiking card.

Trial 3: Corliss says, "Touch hiking." Josephine touches the hiking card.

Trial 4: Corliss says, "Touch hiking." Josephine touches the hiking card.

Trial 5: Corliss says, "Touch hiking." Josephine touches the hiking card.

> Once Josephine masters "touch hiking" after a specified number of sessions, such as two consecutive sessions, of reaching an established criterion, such as scoring at least 80%, the hiking card is placed on the table with pictures of tennis, basketball, soccer, baseball, and swimming, or other mastered recreation activities. The number of cards in the array is based on Josephine's skills or the size of the table.

A positional prompt can be used when introducing the card with the other cards that have been previously mastered by the participant. A *positional prompt* is a target card placed slightly closer to the individual than the array of other mastered cards.

> For example, after completing two sessions when Josephine correctly identified "hiking" 80% of the time, the positional prompt is faded and all cards are placed the same distance from Josephine. Corliss then randomly asks Josephine to provide him with different cards in the array. If hiking continues to be correctly identified with 80% accuracy after two sessions then the concept of hiking is considered mastered and new concepts can continue to be introduced in this manner.

148

Now it is time for you to apply this information.

1. Identify an *additional recreation activity* that you might teach Josephine:

_____

2. Describe how you will introduce this concept to Josephine using **random rotation**:

_____

_____

_____

3. Describe how you will introduce this concept to Josephine using **expanded trials**.

_____

_____

_____

4. Describe how you will introduce this concept to Josephine using **positional prompts**.

_____

_____

_____

Now review your answers.
- For the random rotation example, did you have Josephine identify the new concept in five trials and a mastered concept in five trials?
- For the expanded trials example, did you use mass trials to introduce a new concept?
- For the positional prompt example, did you place the new card slightly in front of the other cards?

Differentiating between concepts is one type of discrimination training. Another type of discrimination training teaches individuals to adapt to different situations or circumstances. **Stimulus discrimination** might be helpful for leisure service professionals who are providing numerous activities that result in having a variety of scheduled programs and limited resources with a large number of participants. *Stimulus discrimination* is a process that is used to teach individuals to differentiate between situational cues. For example, one visual cue, a red card, might indicate it is time to take a safety break while a second visual cue, a green card, might indicate it is time to swim.

> For instance, if Talia expresses a preference to use the playground equipment often and at times is required to share some equipment, such as a swing, with other participants for a specified amount of time; stimulus discrimination can help her learn to determine what times it is acceptable to use the playground.

Two techniques used in stimulus discrimination are called:

- response restriction
- multiple schedules

Response restriction is sometimes called *simultaneous discrimination training* because an individual can choose between an appropriate response and a distraction response at the same time. The appropriate response might be a pictorial request to use the playground and the distraction response might be a blank card. These cards are available to the individual when it is acceptable for the person to make the request and the cards are not available when it is unacceptable for the individual to make a request. Response restriction involves the opportunity for an individual to make a request during a specified time that is not provided continuously; thus, the person is restricted to those responses that are deemed to be acceptable at a particular time.

> For example, Judy might enjoy going for a walk outside but can only do so when an employee or volunteer is available to accompany her. A staff member might place a picture of the walking trail on the front desk when someone is available to accompany Judy outside.

Multiple schedules are sometimes called successive stimuli training because the opportunity to request the desired activity occurs after a period of time when the option is not available. When using multiple schedules one card involving a pictorial request of an activity is presented throughout a session. There is an indicator card, such as a card displaying a traffic light with the green light on, that notifies the participant about the time when a request can be made that will be followed by a response.

> For example, Abu is in a session for 20 minutes when a green card is displayed and he is permitted to request to go to the playground at any point during those 20 minutes. If he makes such an appeal, his request will be granted. When those 20 minutes have elapsed, a red card will be presented. When the red card is displayed Abu is expected to engage in a different activity, such as practicing playing a musical instrument.

When multiple schedules are used, the individual is allowed to make a request; however, the service provider may not always be able to respond to the request.
Now that information about stimulus discrimination has been presented, it is time for you to describe a time when you are conducting a leisure program and might not be able to respond to a request of an individual:

_____

_____

_____

How do you indicate to the individual that you cannot honor a request at that time?

_____

_____

- When reflecting on these questions did you identify situations when participants need to discriminate and differentiate between situations?
- Did you identify an indicator that would be easily identified by the participant?
- How will you teach the participant to discriminate between the stimuli?

In summary, this chapter contains information about ways to teach participants to discriminate between ideas, activities, and situations. A person can be supported to discriminate between concepts through random rotation and expanded trials. The leisure service professional can help an individual discriminate between situations and circumstances through response restriction and multiple schedules.

Now it is time to test your knowledge on the following pages.

Test Your Knowledge of Promoting Discrimination

1. What is the process of analysis that helps an individual to make distinctions between situations called?

    a. activity
    b. discrete
    c. discrimination
    d. sequence
    e. task

2. The process of teaching an individual to differentiate between concepts is called:

    a. discrete training.
    b. discrimination training.
    c. discriminative control.
    d. stimulus discrimination.
    e. stimulus training.

3. What is the process of teaching an individual an appropriate time to make a request called?

    a. discrete training
    b. discrimination training
    c. discriminative control
    d. stimulus discrimination
    e. stimulus training

4. The processes used to expand or assess an individual's understanding of skills or concepts is:

    a. activity analysis and task analysis.
    b. discrimination training and discrete trials.
    c. extinction and punishment.
    d. functional and behavioral assessment.
    e. reinforcement and processing.

5. Which is NOT a method used to expand knowledge or skills?

    a. expanded trials
    b. positional prompts
    c. random rotation
    d. response cost
    e. stimulus discrimination

6. The process that involves the alternating presentation of two previously mastered concepts is called:

    a. expanded trials.
    b. positional prompts.
    c. random rotation.
    d. response cost.
    e. stimulus discrimination.

7. What is the process that involves using discrete trials to introduce a new concept called?

    a. expanded trials
    b. positional prompts
    c. random rotation
    d. response cost
    e. stimulus discrimination

8. The type of prompt used when Haley places a targeted item slightly closer to Ramsey than other items is called:

    a. model
    b. physical
    c. positional
    d. verbal
    e. visual

9. Ling is asked to identify a picture of a swimming pool, then a picture of a park, and then a picture of a swimming pool in a session. This is an example of:

    a. expanded trials.
    b. positional prompts.
    c. random rotation.
    d. response cost.
    e. stimulus discrimination.

10. Jarrell already can identify a paintbrush, paint tube, and pallet. To determine if he can recognize an easel, a picture of an easel is placed in an array with other items. This is an example of:

    a. expanded trials.
    b. positional prompts.
    c. random rotation.
    d. response cost.
    e. stimulus discrimination.

11. Roland is trying to learn when it is appropriate to listen to music. Evelyn places a green card on the table when it is acceptable to play music, and a red card when it is not. This is an example of:

    a. multiple schedules.
    b. positional prompts.
    c. random rotation.
    d. response restriction.
    e. stimulus discrimination.

12. Alfonzo places a picture of a swimming pool and a blank card on the refrigerator whenever it is an appropriate time for Robin to ask him to go swimming. This is an example of:

    a. multiple schedules.
    b. positional prompts.
    c. random rotation.
    d. response restriction.
    e. stimulus discrimination.

13. The opportunity to request a desired activity after a period of time when the option is not available is referred to as:

    a. multiple schedules.
    b. positional prompts.
    c. random rotation.
    d. response restriction.
    e. stimulus discrimination.

14. What is response restriction sometimes called?

    a. expanded trials
    b. multiple schedules
    c. random rotation
    d. simultaneous discrimination
    e. successive stimuli

15. Jeremy likes to kick the soccer ball repeatedly in the air. During soccer practice, Angie puts a red flag in her pocket when Jeremy is not permitted to kick the soccer ball in the air. This is an example of:

    a. discrete training.
    b. discrimination training.
    c. discriminative control.
    d. stimulus discrimination.
    e. stimulus training.

After completing the evaluation, please check your answers with those recorded in the back of the book. When you are satisfied with the knowledge you have acquired, please turn the page and begin work on the next chapter.

19 GENERALIZE BEHAVIORS

One of the major criticisms of behavior analysis procedures is the inability of individuals whose behaviors have been changed by these procedures to exhibit their newly acquired behaviors in different environments and under different circumstances. Exhibiting newly acquired behaviors in different environments and circumstances is referred to as generalization.

Generalization involves the exhibition of a target behavior:

- over time,

- in a variety of situations or settings,

- across different individuals, and

- with similar materials.

Generalization can also involve the demonstration of various related behaviors that are similar to the target behavior. Because generalization of skills does not often occur automatically, systematic procedures should be employed that encourage generalization. Therefore, a requirement of a training procedure should be the exhibition of target behaviors during conditions outside of the training situation.

One way to encourage generalization, which has previously been addressed in this text, is the idea of **intermittent reinforcement**. Remember that the systematic occasional delivery of reinforcers increases the likelihood that a behavior will be maintained. *Maintenance* of a behavior is the aspect of generalization that is concerned with the exhibition of a target behavior over time.

Once a participant in a leisure program has learned a behavior, the practitioner gradually decreases the amount and rate that the reinforcer is being administered. As the practitioner decreases the reinforcer, the participant is required to exhibit more of the desired behavior for a longer period of time to receive the same amount of reinforcement.

> For example, when teaching Moesha to play basketball, the coach, David, praises her each time she completes a pass to a teammate (a fixed ratio of 1:1). After she successfully learns this skill, David decides to reinforce her on the average of every four times she completes a pass during practice (a variable ratio of 4:1). As her skills increase David then reinforces her on the average of every 10 passes she completes (a variable ratio of 10:1).

In the previous example, the basketball coach systematically reduced the amount of reinforcement delivered, while increasing the frequency of the desired behavior. The systematic reduction or introduction of reinforcement or punishment is termed **fading**. *Fading* involves the gradual change of the antecedent or consequence of a behavior in order to encourage a behavior to occur in response to a partial or new antecedent or consequence. The procedure of fading can be actively used to teach a variety of leisure skills.

> For instance, Vanessa, a leisure service professional, is attempting to teach Sanchez, who is an active young man with motor coordination problems, how to paint a picture. In preparation, Vanessa traces a picture on an easel paper. Vanessa then places a paintbrush in Sanchez's hand and physically guides his hand so that he paints the picture. After several teaching trials, Vanessa begins to fade the pressure of her hand as the signal for painting. Vanessa accomplishes this fading procedure by (a) lightly holding Sanchez's hand for several trials; then (b) touching her fingertips to the back of his hand for additional trials; then (c) pointing to the picture, and finally (d) simply giving Sanchez the easel, paint, and paint brush. Once Sanchez is successfully painting the picture, the amount of the picture traced on the paper can also be systematically reduced (faded).

The fading examples above should sound somewhat familiar. The fading procedure is similar to that of shaping. However, there is a definite difference between the two strategies. Remember that *shaping* involves the reinforcement of successive approximations of a target behavior so that the demonstrated behavior gradually resembles the target behavior. When applying the shaping procedure, the behavior is changed. Fading involves the gradual changing of the antecedents or consequences while the behavior is maintained. Therefore, the application of the shaping procedure allows leisure service delivery professionals to initially teach a skill to their clientele, while fading facilitates generalization of these leisure skills.

Factors Influencing Generalization

The likelihood of generalization depends on various circumstances that include the following:

- **Teach in a context as similar as possible to the context in which the behavior is ultimately to be performed.**
- **Use reinforcers that are naturally occurring in the environment.**
- **Attempt to use the pairing procedure.**

The more similar two situations, people, or materials are, the more likely it is that the behavior will generalize. Therefore, one way to encourage generalization is to **teach in a context as similar as possible to the environment in which the behavior is ultimately to be performed**.

> For instance, a leisure service professional wants to encourage individuals to attend recreation activities in the community by teaching people to use the mass transit system. The likelihood of generalization of the skill to a variety of different buses would be increased if the training actually occurred on a bus, rather than in a large cardboard replica of a bus placed in a gymnasium.

Another factor that affects the ability of an individual to generalize the behavior involves the type of reinforcer used during the initial educational session. If the reinforcers used during the teaching session are not available in other situations, the likelihood of generalization is then reduced. Therefore, whenever possible while teaching, **use reinforcers that are naturally occurring in the environment** (typically secondary reinforcers such as social interaction and activity involvement).

A problem arises when professionals are unable to identify any reinforcers other than primary items for some of their clientele. In such a situation, the professional may **attempt to use the pairing procedure**. *Pairing* involves the coupling together of two antecedents or consequences in an attempt to have one begin to assume the properties of the other.

> For example, Renaldo, a leisure service professional, is attempting to encourage Shiloh, who has returned home from a serious accident, to practice walking. He observed that Shiloh only walks when she is given some candy. Renaldo decides to use candy to reward Shiloh for walking. However, each time he gives Shiloh candy, he also administers social praise. He continues to pair the two consequences together in an attempt to have the social praise assume the reinforcing properties of the candy. Once the pairing has continued for a time Renaldo gradually fades the candy while continuing his verbal praise. Finally, Shiloh is only receiving social praise for practicing her walking. The work of Renaldo is not yet over. He now begins to fade his social praise until Shiloh is independently practicing walking.

Complete the following exercise related to the application of generalization principles.

Directions: Answer the questions based on the following paragraph.

You have decided to improve the William's swimming skills so that he can independently use his community swimming pool. Currently, you are providing him with verbal praise each time he swims a complete width of the pool. To enable William to successfully reach the opposite side of the pool, you hold his stomach and provide him with physical prompts to move his arms, legs, and head correctly.

1. How might you fade the assistance you are providing William?

    _____

    _____

    _____

2. What other reinforcer, that is more natural, could you pair with verbal praise?

    _____

    _____

    _____

3. How might you apply the idea of intermittent reinforcement in an attempt to have William maintain his swimming skills?

    _____

    _____

    _____

4. Where would be the ideal place to teach William to swim?

    _____

    _____

    _____

Now, turn the page to review your answers.

If your answers resemble the following, you are gaining insight related to the concept of generalization.

1. How might you fade the assistance you are presently providing William? Gradually remove the physical prompts to move his arms, legs, and head by replacing them with gestural cues and then allowing him to perform them independently. Subtly reduce the amount of pressure on his stomach with your hand. Now that you are no longer touching him, you could first simply stand beside him and then you could gradually move away until you are watching from the deck.

2. What other reinforcer that is more natural could you pair with verbal praise? Placing his hand on the opposite end of the pool.

3. How might you apply the idea of intermittent reinforcement in an attempt to have William maintain his swimming skills? When he is able to successfully swim one width with regularity, begin reinforcing him after he completes an average of two widths (variable ratio). If he continues to show progress, move to a variable ratio of four laps per reinforcer. Continue this process by making him perform more while receiving less reinforcement.

4. Where would be the ideal place to teach William to swim? The ideal place is the local community swimming pool that is frequented by his peers.

Consider these guidelines for generalization:

*   **Use intermittent reinforcement.**
*   **Gradually fade reinforcers that are maintaining the target behavior.**
*   **Teach in an environment similar to where the target behavior is to occur.**
*   **Whenever possible, use naturally occurring reinforcers.**
*   **If unnatural reinforcers are used, pair them with natural reinforcers.**

While considering these guidelines, please turn to the next page to test your knowledge of generalization.

Test Your Knowledge of Generalizing Behaviors

1. Generalization refers to a behavior that:

   a. automatically occurs in a given situation.
   b. has been established in one situation and, as a result, occurs more readily in other situations.
   c. is an approximation of the target behavior.
   d. is generally appropriate for any situation.
   e. occurs more readily in one situation than in any other situation.

2. Maintenance of a behavior refers to a behavior that:

   a. cannot generalize from one situation to another.
   b. does not occur outside of a training session.
   c. does not require reinforcement.
   d. is exhibited over a span of time in a variety of settings.
   e. quickly extinguishes outside of a training session.

3. To facilitate maintenance of behavior, reinforcement should be delivered:

   a. consecutively.
   b. continuously.
   c. generally.
   d. intermittently.
   e. sequentially.

4. To facilitate generalization of a behavior, reinforcement should be delivered:

   a. consecutively.
   b. continuously.
   c. generally.
   d. intermittently.
   e. sequentially.

5. Fading is:

   a. a procedure used to eliminate an inappropriate behavior.
   b. the discouragement of intermittent reinforcement.
   c. the gradual diminishing of a target behavior.
   d. the planned introduction or lessening of reinforcement or punishment.
   e. the weakening of the intensity of a reinforcer.

6. Fading is a procedure that:

   a. can be used to influence either the antecedent or the consequence of a behavior.
   b. can only be used to influence the antecedent of a behavior.
   c. can only be used to influence the consequence of a behavior.
   d. has limited application; that is, it can only be used in a small number of situations.
   e. is more effective with a fixed ratio reinforcement schedule than a variable ratio schedule.

7. Shaping and fading are alike in that:

   a. a general resemblance of a behavior to the target behavior is all that is required for success with either procedure.
   b. both procedures involve gradual change.
   c. both procedures require fixed ratio schedules of reinforcement.
   d. both procedures require variable ratio schedules of reinforcement.
   e. both procedures use successive approximations of the target behavior.

8. Shaping and fading are different in that shaping involves:

   a. gradual changing of a behavior and fading involves gradual changing of the antecedent or consequence of a behavior.
   b. gradual changing of the antecedent of a behavior and fading involves gradual changing of the consequence of a behavior.
   c. gradual changing of the antecedents or consequences of a behavior and fading involves changing of the behavior.
   d. gradual changing of the consequence of a behavior and fading involves gradual changing of the antecedent of a behavior.
   e. punishment and fading involves reinforcement.

9. Generalization of a behavior is more likely to occur if the:

   a. natural environment provides continuous reinforcement.
   b. training environment and the natural environment are not alike.
   c. training environment and the natural environment are similar.
   d. training environment provides continuous reinforcement.
   e. training environment offers opportunities for fading and the natural environment offers opportunities for shaping.

10. Generalization of a behavior is more likely to occur if the reinforcers used in the training sessions are:

    a. also available in the natural environment.
    b. also used in the shaping procedure.
    c. continuous.
    d. only available during the training sessions.
    e. used in a variable ratio schedule of reinforcement.

11. Pairing involves the joining of

    a. an antecedent with a consequence to promote generalization.
    b. continuous and intermittent reinforcement.
    c. fading and continuous reinforcement to promote generalization.
    d. the procedures of fading and shaping to promote generalization.
    e. two antecedents or consequences of a behavior so that one will take on the characteristics and effects of the other.

12. Pairing involves the joining of a:

    a. primary reinforcer with another primary reinforcer.
    b. primary reinforcer with an intermittent reinforcer.
    c. secondary reinforcer with a fixed ratio schedule of reinforcement.
    d. secondary reinforcer with a primary reinforcer.
    e. secondary reinforcer with a variable ratio schedule of reinforcement.

13. Which of the following is considered to be a strategy to follow in an attempt to promote generalization?

    a. Gradually fade reinforcers that are maintaining the target behavior.
    b. Train in an environment similar to where the target behavior is to occur.
    c. Use continuous reinforcement.
    d. When primary reinforcers are used, pair them with natural reinforcers.
    e. Whenever possible, use naturally occurring reinforcers.

14. If Rashid, a leisure service professional, implements a carefully planned process of reducing the amount of reinforcement used to sustain a behavior, Rashid is:

    a. following a variable schedule of reinforcement.
    b. generalizing.
    c. intermittently reinforcing.
    d. using a fading procedure.
    e. using an extinction procedure.

15. If Margret uses food as a reinforcer of a behavior and links verbal praise with the food, the verbal praise becomes:

    a. a conditioned reinforcer.
    b. a generalized reinforcer.
    c. a token reinforcer.
    d. an intermittent reinforcer.
    e. an unnatural reinforcer.

Now that you have completed the evaluation, please check your answers with the ones listed in the back of the book. If needed, review the material and try the exercises again. If you are satisfied with your retention of the material, congratulations are definitely in order.

20 SUPPORT POSITIVE BEHAVIORS

Typically, people participate in recreation activities to have fun and enjoy themselves. Often, participants cooperate effectively with one another to create a positive experience. Unfortunately, at times, some participants engage in behaviors that infringe on the ability of other participants to experience leisure. To maximize the occurrence of behaviors conducive to leisure and minimize the occurrence of problem behaviors in leisure contexts, it is often helpful to use approaches that are similar to those used in other settings, such as at home. It is also helpful for leisure service providers to use strategies across program settings.

One way to promote consistent practices is the use of a concept known as **positive behavioral supports** or positive behavioral interventions and supports. The approach of *positive behavioral supports* includes a systematic, agency wide, process used to support behaviors of all individuals who attend a particular agency. The use of positive behavioral supports occurs at three levels.

The *primary level* is inclusive of the entire agency involving stipulation of strategies and techniques used throughout the agency by all personnel. These procedures are designed to encourage positive behaviors and address behaviors that create problems in people having positive experiences. At this primary level, the use of positive behavioral supports includes a description of the overall assessment process. This process is used to identify behavioral expectations and describe strategies to be used for improving, preventing, maintaining, and altering behaviors. The goal of positive behavioral support at the primary level is to create a culture that promotes positive behaviors and, as a result, reduces the incidence of behaviors that create problems for the individual and group.

> An example of a positive behavioral support system with children includes the expectation that participants have "listening ears," use "kind words," and have "quiet hands and feet" during activities that occur within the recreation center. Another example of a positive behavioral support system that can be implemented with children involves the use of a specific token economy.

The wording for participant expectations focuses on identifying and encouraging positive behaviors instead of decreasing negative behaviors. For example:

Positive Behaviors	Negative Behaviors
Speaks at acceptable volume	No screaming
Respects other's property	No stealing
Has Quiet feet	No kicking, running
Speaks at acceptable times	No interrupting

For each of the following negative behaviors, identify a positive alternative.

1. Swears or curses: _____

2. Rolls on the ground: _____

3. Hordes possessions: _____

4. Hits self: _____

5. Does not follow instructions: _____

Did your answers focus on the positive behaviors that you hope to see, such as:

- uses respectful words
- walks and remains upright
- shares belongings
- plays with toys
- follows instructions

The **secondary level** of a positive behavioral support system addresses potential behaviors that occur with each participant. At this level, the leisure service professional will teach skills necessary for individuals to be successful. This approach is focused on promoting positive behaviors and preventing problem behaviors.

> For example, leisure education sessions might be offered to increase decision-making and problem-solving skills as well as to promote awareness of available leisure resources. The agency may also offer programs designed to manage stress and anger and thereby prevent problem behaviors. All of the opportunities are intended to teach participants about expectations while they are present at the recreation center.

For each of the target behaviors listed identify a recreation activity that can be a context in which the skills can be taught and rewarded.

1. Follow directions: _____

2. Use respectful words:_____

3. Keep hands to self: _____

4. Keep feet to self: _____

5. Walk with staff:_____

While reflecting on your answers above, consider if your activities required use of the target behaviors, such as these:

- Using the games *Mother May I* or *Name that Tune* can require participants to follow directions.
- Playing *Warm Fuzzy Bags* where participants write something kind about each person in a group can provide opportunities to use words that are respectful.
- Watching videos about people complimenting others can be used to teach people to use kind words.
- Doing parallel activities, such as coloring or painting, can provide opportunities for participants to practice using their hands in a constructive manner.
- Playing *Freeze Tag* might be used to have participants use their feet in an appropriate way.
- Playing *Follow the Leader* might encourage participants to walk upright.

The **tertiary level** of a positive behavioral support system is used to complement the instructional system designed to teach participants knowledge and skills within a leisure context. This tertiary level helps support behaviors that are conducive for success and promote leisure as well as address behaviors that are disruptive to the leisure context and are creating problems for that person and other participants trying to experience leisure. At this level, a **functional behavioral assessment** is conducted and an individualized behavior plan is developed. A *functional behavioral assessment* is used to assess behaviors surrounding the occurrence of behaviors that encourage leisure and problem behaviors to ascertain:

- when the behaviors occurs,
- what might be stimulating the behaviors, and
- what are the consequences of the behaviors.

Functional behavioral assessments are a formal means to address the antecedents, behaviors, and consequences discussed in Chapter 8. Functional behavior assessments are a method of documenting the sequence so that all staff can analyze an individual's behavior patterns. In the tertiary level, service providers employ sequence analysis to identify when participants engage in "positive behaviors" so that these behaviors are systematically rewarded. Sequence analysis is also used to determine when participants engage in "negative behaviors" so that a plan is established to encourage the replacement of negative behaviors with "positive behaviors."

An example of a functional behavioral assessment used for Anthony who is enrolled at a day camp might be as follows:

Time of Day	Antecedent	Behavior	Consequence
9:00-9:29	Parent says "good bye"	Cries (5min)	Receives attention from staff
9:30-9:59		N/A	
10:00-10:29		N/A	
10:30-10:59	Staff prepares snack	Grabs staff arm 3x	Obtains desired item
11:00-11:29		N/A	
11:29-11:59		N/A	
12:00-12:29	Moves from playground to lunch area	Kicks staff 5x	Escapes staff request to go inside
12:30-12:59		N/A	
1:00-1:29		N/A	
1:30-1:59	Moves from swimming pool to art area	Kicks staff 4x	Escapes staff request to leave swimming pool
2:00-2:29		N/A	
2:30-3:00	Waits for ride	Grabs staff arm 4x	Receives attention from staff

After evaluating the behaviors involved in the situation, a **functional behavioral plan** is identified to increase the number of positive behaviors that are incompatible with a behavior that is disruptive. An increase in these positive behaviors should help to prevent or reduce the number of behaviors creating problems.

After examining results of the example of the tertiary functional behavioral assessment, it can be seen that behaviors that are disruptive to the situation tend to occur most frequently during times when participants are moving from one location to another or are sitting and waiting for the next activity to begin. As a result, some form of immediate reinforcement for positive behaviors, such as use of electronics, might be helpful as Anthony moves to the next location or is waiting for the upcoming activity to begin.

The functional behavioral plan describes strategies designed to teach positive behaviors that result in enjoyable engagement and to reduce the occurrence of behaviors that disrupt the opportunity for participants to learn and experience leisure. Contained in the behavior plan are **goals** identified to increase positive behaviors and decrease negative behaviors.

The behavior plan also describes **strategies** to be used to increase the occurrence of positive behaviors and decrease negative ones. Goals are based on the functional behavior analysis and responses are recorded to monitor changes in the individual's behavior pattern over the course of a program.

The behavioral plan includes all **documentation** used by leisure service professionals. This documentation is reviewed on a regular, systematic schedule, such as monthly or quarterly, to determine if changes are needed to the behavioral plan. Specific words or phrases that staff members use to encourage the individual to perform tasks are included in the plan. The behavior plan includes any information that increases awareness of other staff members about behaviors to display when interacting with the individual that tend to increase positive behaviors while reducing those behaviors that create problems for that individual and other people in the situation.

In summary, the behavioral plan includes the following three components:

- goals

- strategies

- documentation

> For example, in Anthony's behavior assessment, we find that he enjoys listening to music, and while doing so smiles and speaks with others. The behavior assessment also indicates that he tends to grab others. This form of aggression typically occurs most during transitions from a highly preferred activity to a less preferred activity. The goal might be to reduce the number of times Anthony grabs others by 80% after six weeks. To achieve this goal, the service providers might plan to use another highly preferred activity, such as listening to music, to reward Anthony for interacting in a positive manner with others for a specified duration while he transitions to another activity.

Now, it is time for you to develop a functional behavior plan for Tabia.

Time of Day	Antecedent	Behavior	Consequence
9:00-9:29	Parent says "good bye"	Cries for 5 min	Attention from staff
9:30-9:59		N/A	
10:00-10:29		N/A	
10:30-10:59	Staff leaves to prepare snack	Cries for 5 min	Attention from staff
11:00-11:29		N/A	
11:29-11:59		N/A	
12:00-12:29	Staff pushes another child on swing	Cries for 3 min	Attention from staff
12:30-12:59		N/A	
1:00-1:29		N/A	
1:30-1:59		N/A	
2:00-2:29		N/A	
2:30-3:00	Staff leaves to make copies	Grabs staff arm 4x	Attention from staff

1. Write a **goal** designed to increase a positive behavior demonstrated by Tabia that is incompatible with a disruptive behavior:

   _____

   _____

   _____

2. Identify a **strategy** to increase a positive behavior demonstrated by Tabia that is incompatible with a disruptive behavior:

   _____

   _____

   _____

Reflect on your answers for this activity using the following questions.

- Did the goal associated with increasing Tabia's positive behaviors involve increasing her ability to wait quietly for assistance?
- Did your strategies include providing reinforcement of behavior incompatible with crying and grabbing others?

In summary, at the tertiary level, the leisure service professional:

1. Conducts a **functional behavioral assessment**
2. Develops and implements **the functional behavioral plan.**

Overall, this chapter examined the role of positive behavior supports in leisure contexts. A positive behavioral support system occurs at three levels:

1. **Primary**: Agency-wide policies and procedures for teaching participants by encouraging and increasing positive behaviors and prevent and reduce problem behaviors.
2. **Secondary**: The programs and services offered by the agency to individuals to encourage and increase positive behaviors and prevent or reduce problem behaviors.
3. **Tertiary**: The specific individualized plan for participants that is designed to encourage and increase positive behaviors and prevent or reduce problem behaviors.

Now test your knowledge on the following pages.

Test Your Knowledge of Supporting Positive Behaviors

1. This is a systematic, agency-wide process used to support behavior of all individuals at an agency:

   a. applied behavior analysis
   b. behavior intervention plans
   c. positive behavioral supports
   d. positive behavioral plan
   e. strategic behavior plan

2. This level of positive behavioral supports includes programs, such as stress management, to teach and encourage "positive behaviors":

   a. primary level
   b. secondary level
   c. tertiary level
   d. all of the above
   e. none of the above

3. This level of positive behavioral supports involves a functional behavioral assessment.

   a. primary level
   b. secondary level
   c. tertiary level
   d. all of the above
   e. none of the above

4. This level of positive behavioral supports involves development of a functional behavioral plan:

   a. primary level
   b. secondary level
   c. tertiary level
   d. all of the above
   e. none of the above

5. This level of positive behavioral supports involves identifying agency-wide policies and procedures:

   a. primary level
   b. secondary level
   c. tertiary level
   d. all of the above
   e. none of the above

6. The following positive statement could be used as a substitute for the negative statement "no hitting staff":

   a. It is nice that you use kind words.
   b. It is thoughtful that you listen quietly.
   c. It is helpful that your feet remain close to you.
   d. Thank you for keeping your hands close to you.
   e. I appreciate you waiting your turn to speak.

7. Which of the following positive statement would replace "no swearing"?

    a. It is nice that you use kind words.
    b. It is thoughtful that you listen quietly.
    c. It is helpful that your feet remain close to you.
    d. Thank you for keeping your hands close to you.
    e. I appreciate you waiting your turn to speak.

8. Antecedents, behaviors, and consequences are analyzed in which of the following processes?

    a. applied behavior analysis
    b. behavior intervention plans
    c. functional behavioral assessment
    d. positive behavioral plan
    e. strategic behavior plan

9. The YMCA develops a policy that staff will give participants a token each time the staff see a participant "complimenting another participant." This occurs at what level of a positive behavior support?

    a. primary level
    b. secondary level
    c. tertiary level
    d. all of the above
    e. none of the above

10. Gabrielle usually yells when she remains seated for more than 10 minutes. When she yells, staff come to her and speak with her quietly. In this example, the act of yelling is the:

    a. antecedent.
    b. affidavit.
    c. behavior.
    d. consequence.
    e. conversion.

11. Gabrielle usually yells when she remains seated for more than 10 minutes. When she yells staff come to her and speak with her quietly. In this example, approaching Gabrielle and speaking to her is the:

    a. antecedent.
    b. affidavit.
    c. behavior.
    d. consequence.
    e. conversion.

12. Gabrielle usually yells when she remains seated for more than 10 minutes. When she yells staff come to her and speak with her quietly. In this example, sitting in her seat for at least 10 minutes the:

    a. antecedent.
    b. affidavit.
    c. behavior.
    d. consequence.
    e. conversion.

13. When working on a craft project, Jorge hits Valencia to get her to help him with the project. In this example, hitting is the:

    a. antecedent.
    b. affidavit.
    c. behavior.
    d. consequence.
    e. conversion.

14. When working on a craft project, Jorge hits Valencia to get her to help him with the project. In this example, Valencia working on the craft project is the:

    a. antecedent.
    b. affidavit.
    c. behavior.
    d. consequence.
    e. conversion.

15. When working on a craft project, Jorge hits Valencia to get her to help him with the project. In this example, giving Jorge help is the:

    a. antecedent.
    b. affidavit.
    c. behavior.
    d. consequence.
    e. conversion.

After completing the evaluation, please check your answers with those recorded in the back of the book. When you are satisfied with the knowledge you have acquired, please turn the page and begin work on the next chapter.

21 USE EVIDENCE-BASED PRACTICE

Throughout this book we have discussed how the principles of behavior analysis complement leisure service delivery in terms of assessment, planning, implementation, evaluation, and documentation. Accountability and quality assurance are important considerations when providing any human service. These concerns have led to development of the concept of "evidence-based practice," or similar concepts such as "benefits-based programming," and "best practices." *Evidence-based practice* is the process that occurs when professionals design programs based on specific techniques that are demonstrated to be effective by research studies. These programs are then used to meet specific goals or objectives.

The inference of evidenced based practice is that it is critical to demonstrate that services are effective and have value. Professionals involved in service delivery access and support use of evidence based practice by becoming familiar with or helping to conduct relevant research examining intervention efficacy. In this context, *efficacy* involves the ability or capacity of a program or approach to produce a positive impact on a person or people's behaviors and, ultimately, their lives. It is also valuable if professionals involved in conducting research attempt to answer questions that address important personal and social problems and work to identify possible solutions to these problems.

Results of research identifying evidenced based practice can be used in all phases of programming. For example, information can be systematically collected and evaluated to determine if a person's behaviors that facilitate positive leisure engagement have improved or if a specific teaching strategy is working. Also, research that delineates evidenced based practice can be used in program planning and implementation by: helping to identify procedures that have been successful, determining appropriate session lengths, and understanding ways to access program materials.

Determining evidence-based practice is more than merely using research in practice. Use of evidence-based practice also involves critically evaluating research to determine best practices.

An example of an identified evidence-based practice is presented in Buettner and Fitzsimmons' Dementia Practice Guidelines. In addition to positive behaviors such as holding someone's hand or complimenting another person, the authors identified challenging behaviors exhibited by individuals who have dementia such as wandering, limited positive affect such as smiling or laughing, and behaviors demonstrating aggression such as verbally or physically assaulting another person. Buettner and Fitzsimmons reviewed the literature on programs such as a wheelchair biking programs, sensory stimulation procedures, and social groups that are all designed to increase positive behaviors and decrease negative ones. The authors examined the frequency and types of research used to determine if a program reduced a targeted negative behavior; they then assigned a grade to each intervention to identify the strongest and weakest approaches. Subsequently, the authors developed evidence-based protocols built on the research.

Research Designs

An understanding of research designs is helpful when making evidence-based decisions. Some common research designs include the following:

- experimental designs
- quasi-experimental designs
- single-case designs
- surveys
- case studies

When using an **experimental design,** a **dependent variable** or multiple dependent variables and an **independent variable** or multiple independent variables are identified. The *dependent variable* is often the target behavior that is being measured while the *independent variable* is often the program used to bring about some change. In a true experimental design, both the independent and dependent variables are controlled and manipulated to minimize the possibility of behavior change occurring as a result of other causes. Often experimental research is done in a laboratory with a pre-test phase that includes collecting baseline data and a post-test phase that measures the dependent variable after the intervention has been presented.

It is helpful when using an experimental design to randomly assign participants to at least two groups, with at least one group receiving the intervention, the *treatment group,* and the other group or groups who do not immediately receive the intervention, often identified as the *wait-list* or *control group. Random assignment* means that participants have the same chance of being included in one group as another. Each group of participants typically possesses similar demographic characteristics, such as age, education level, or socio-economic status. The people who are participants in the research study are identified as the *sample.* The higher the number of people in the sample the better, since one purpose of experiments is to generalize findings from the sample to a population. Data from experimental design studies are often analyzed using statistics.

Quasi-experimental research is similar to experimental research in that these studies often meet most of the criteria of an experimental research design but not all. These studies might only include examination of one group with research conducted in a naturally occurring environment where other factors might influence results. Also quasi-experimental studies are used when random assignment to different groups is not feasible.

Single-case designs are based on the repeated measurement of behavior under baseline and intervention conditions. This is commonly referred to as *baseline logic.* It differs from group research design logic in which different groups of individuals are assigned to *either* a control group or an experimental group. With group designs a single individual's behavior is seldom measured repeatedly under both control (baseline) and experimental (intervention) conditions, as it is in single-case research design. With single-case research designs, only a few cases are examined, with repeated measures of variables that may be impacted by the intervention that is systematically applied to each individual. Results are graphically displayed and inferences about relationships between variables are typically determined by visual examination. Each individual, who serves as his or her control, participates in each experimental condition.

One aspect of single-case research designs that can be appealing is their ability to measure behaviors in an applied setting where leisure services are delivered. Within this applied context, single-case research designs can be used to examine effects of interventions. Implementation of this research method can promote effective documentation of leisure service outcomes. Since both leisure service delivery and single-case research designs focus on examining effects of programs on each participant, this method helps meet the individual needs of participants.

Survey research requires asking people questions and recording their responses. A *survey* is a way to collect information. Surveys can be administered via a *questionnaire* that involves presenting the questions or probes in a written form or an *interview* that involves the delivery of questions or probes verbally. *Probes* are statements designed to elicit a verbal response from participants.

Existing surveys can be chosen or they can be developed. There are advantages of using previously developed surveys that have been tested and used previously since they may have been examined relative to the reliability and validity of the results obtained from the measurement instruments. *Reliability* includes the consistency of a measure involving the likelihood that if surveys, assessments, or tests were administered to a person repeatedly that the scores or results achieved would be similar under fairly consistent conditions. *Validity* refers to the ability of surveys, assessments, or tests to accurately reflect what is reportedly being measured. It can also be helpful to construct a survey to meet the specific needs of the situation and people involved.

There are many decisions associated with conducting survey research such as identifying the:

- **types** of questions asked,
- **content** of the questions,
- **wording** of the questions,
- **sequence** of questions, and
- **manner** in which participants will respond.

Case studies are a type of research used to conduct an in-depth examination of an individual, a small group of people, or an entire group. Information collected for a case study typically occurs over an extended period of time. Techniques to collect data for case studies include observations, interviews, examination of records, and collections of writing samples. The intent of case studies is to examine something in such detail that it provides insights into the particular individual or group that is being studied that may be relevant to other people or situations. Case studies can be:

- **explanatory** that helps to determine why something occurs.
- **exploratory** that helps to identify new information associated with a topic.
- **descriptive** that explains a situation, group, or context.

A case study is often *prospective,* involving the observation of a person or group; however, a case study can also be *retrospective,* requiring examination of historical information.

Criteria for Evidenced-Based Practices

Governmental and advocacy groups, such as the Centers for Disease Control and National Autism Center also identify "best practices." For example, The National Professional Development Center on Autism Spectrum Disorders (NPDC-ASD) defined Evidence-Based Practice as the following:

- two high-quality experimental or quasi-experimental group design studies, or
- five high-quality single case design studies conducted by at least three different investigators or research groups, or
- one high-quality randomized or quasi-experimental group design study and three high-quality single case designs conducted by at least three different investigators.

Using these criteria, the NPDC-ASD identified 24 "best practices" for working with people who have autism spectrum disorders. Many of these "best practices" use techniques described in this book. For example, the chapters contain guidelines for the application of positive reinforcement and discrete trials and parts of chapters provide recommendations on ways to provide differential reinforcement, extinction, functional behavior assessment, functional communication training, prompting, and picture exchange communication system. These techniques have been identified as "best practices." There are numerous examples contained in professional journals that describe the manner in which some of other techniques identified on the list of best practices are used in leisure contexts.

It is important for professionals who deliver health, education, and leisure services to know how to access and use research to inform and guide their practice. By using measurement techniques outlined in this book, systematic and informed decisions are made associated with service delivery. When leisure service professionals gather information that demonstrate measureable outcomes and then structure their programs based on research published in relevant journals they are using evidence-based practice.

Now it is time for you to practice applying some of the material that has been presented. Use *Google Scholar*, *Google*, and other search engines or examine some relevant professional journals to locate a recent study that illustrates the use of the following five types of research designs. Record the title of the article in the space provided:

1. Single case design: _____

    _____

    _____

    _____

2. Survey: _____

    _____

    _____

    _____

3. Experimental design: _____

    _____

    _____

    _____

4. Case study: _____

    _____

    _____

    _____

5. Quasi-experimental: _____

    _____

    _____

    _____

Some questions that might be helpful to answer while reviewing the studies include the following:

- What types of programs, procedures, or interventions were used in the study?
- If no programs, procedures, or interventions were used, what variables were examined?
- What measurements were used to determine relationships between variables or the impact of the program, procedure, or intervention?
- What did you learn from the study that you could use to improve services you provide?

Procedures for Conducting Evidenced-Based Practice

As mentioned at the beginning of the chapter, for professionals to **be a member of a research team** is an ideal way to contribute to the evidence that substantiates various programs and practices. In addition, the use of evidenced-based practice can be promoted when professionals seek to learn about research examining effects of programs they are currently using or are considering their implementation.

Professionals can **explore databases** to identify and obtain relevant research studies. Such information can be accessed via the Internet by conducting searches using various search engines, such as *Goggle Scholar*. Another way to search databases is to work with a librarian to identify and obtain relevant articles. By including key words associated with procedures, programs, or interventions and, perhaps, particular clientele, professionals can obtain a list of various articles that have been conducted examining effects of such techniques.

An additional way to identify relevant research is to **read peer-reviewed professional journals**. A journal is identified as *peer reviewed* when it implements a procedure that requires colleagues to review a paper prior to publication to decide if it provides suitable content for the journal and contains adequate rigor to be published in the journal. These reviewers, who typically are unaware of the identity of the author(s) of the paper, referred to as a *blind review process*, often provide important and meaningful information to revise and improve the quality of the paper for the readership.

It is one thing to read an article and another to **critically review the literature.** Using *critical thinking* involves clarifying the meaning and significance of what is presented and determining if there is sufficient explanation to accept the reported results. Such critical analysis of research studies and the literature can help professionals determine the most effective procedures to implement.

Once professionals are empowered by the knowledge of research that examines effects of various programs, procedures, and interventions, they are situated to **develop services.** The services that are developed based on the research are then ready to be **implemented.** As a program is implemented, it is helpful to employ an important aspect of evidenced-based practice that is a valuable aspect of the programming process, **evaluate services.** When professionals conduct ongoing evaluations throughout program implementation, known as *formative evaluation*, and *summative evaluations* that include evaluations conducted at the end of a program, they are then prepared to continue to contribute to their knowledge of what might be the most effect services they can offer.

The following activity is a way to practice applying some information presented in this chapter. Explore the literature and determine which of the following recreation activities has the most evidence to support using it to decrease participant pain: aquatics, sports, expressive arts, horseback riding, or tai chi. In the space provided on the next page, list the lead author and date of articles you find for each.

1. Aquatics: _____

_____

_____

2. Sports: _____

_____

_____

3. Creative arts: _____

_____

_____

4. Horseback riding: _____

_____

_____

5. Tai chi: _____

_____

_____

When reflecting on the second learning activity, try to answer the following questions:

- What types of research methods were used?
- What were characteristics of people included in the sample?
- What techniques were used in an attempt to achieve the measured outcomes?
- What was the duration of the sessions and how long was the program administered?
- What were the effects of the program used?
- What did you learn from these studies that may influence the program you offer?

In this chapter, we discussed how evidence based practice can be used in leisure services. The following steps summarize this process.

1. **Be a member** of a research team.
2. **Explore** data bases to find relevant research.
3. **Read** peer-reviewed journals.
4. **Critically review** the literature to determine strongest and weakest approaches.
5. **Develop** leisure programs based on the literature.
6. **Implement** leisure programs based on the literature.
7. **Evaluate** your leisure programs and report findings.

Now it is time for you to test your knowledge with this chapter.

Test Your Knowledge of Using Evidence-Based Practice

1. What is the process whereby leisure professionals design programs based on specific techniques demonstrated to be effective by research studies called?

    a. case study
    b. efficacy research
    c. evaluative-based research
    d. evidence-based practice
    e. theory-based practice

2. This type of research might involve questionnaires or interviews:

    a. case study
    b. experimental design
    c. quasi-experimental design
    d. single case design
    e. survey research

3. This type of research might involve tracking the behaviors of one individual over several weeks:

    a. case study
    b. experimental design
    c. quasi-experimental design
    d. single case design
    e. survey research

4. This type of research might involve describing the processes and procedures used during a specific program at a particular agency:

    a. case study
    b. experimental design
    c. quasi-experimental design
    d. single case design
    e. survey research

5. This type of research involves manipulating independent and dependent variables.

    a. case study
    b. experimental design
    c. quasi-experimental design
    d. single case design
    e. survey research

6. This type of research involves randomly assigning research participants to either a treatment group or a wait list control group:

    a. case study
    b. experimental design
    c. quasi-experimental design
    d. single case design
    e. survey research

7. This process is used to assign research participants to either a treatment group or a wait list control group:

   a. assessment
   b. activity modification
   c. evaluation criteria
   d. random assignment
   e. sampling distribution

8. Libby wants to study the percentage of people who are satisfied with the programs at her facility. What type of research is she likely to do?

   a. case study
   b. experimental design
   c. quasi-experimental design
   d. single case design
   e. survey research

9. SoTang tracks the weight loss of a participant, Lexi, in his kickboxing class. He measures Lexi's weight for five days prior to beginning the program. Next, SoTang measures her every day for six weeks as the program is being conducted. He then measures Lexi's weight five days after the first phase of the program has ended. Finally, he measures her weight every day during the second six weeks of the program. What type of research is SoTang most likely conducting?

   a. case study
   b. experimental design
   c. quasi-experimental design
   d. single case design
   e. survey research

10. Henry describes the assessment, planning, intervention and evaluation procedures used during an equestrian program. What type of research is Henry completing?

    a. case study
    b. experimental design
    c. quasi-experimental design
    d. single case design
    e. survey research

11. Pedro had participants in his yoga class complete a perceived stress scale prior to beginning the program. Some individuals were placed on a wait list and others participated in the yoga program for six weeks. When the program was completed both groups were administered the perceived stress scale a second time and results of the two testing sessions were compared. What type of research is this?

    a. case study
    b. experimental design
    c. quasi-experimental design
    d. single case design
    e. survey research

12. Robert asked all potential participants to identify their favorite type of music via a brief question-naire. This is an example of what type of research?

    a. case study
    b. experimental design
    c. quasi-experimental design
    d. single case design
    e. survey research

13. Tamara asked all the participants in her ceramics class to complete a depression scale before and after the six-week course. What type of research is Tamara using?

    a. case study
    b. experimental design
    c. quasi-experimental design
    d. single case design
    e. survey research

14. Zoey described the process that occurs that facilitates county agencies to meet the leisure needs of young adults. What type of research did she likely conduct?

    a. case study
    b. experimental design
    c. quasi-experimental design
    d. single case design
    e. survey research

15. What type of research is often the least generalizable?

    a. case study
    b. experimental design
    c. quasi-experimental design
    d. single case design
    e. survey research

After completing the evaluation, please check your answers with those recorded in the back of the book. When you are satisfied with the knowledge you have acquired, please turn the page and begin work on the next chapter.

Conclusion

Behavior analysis is a learning process based on the belief that behaviors are developed and changed through the arrangement of environmental conditions that are the antecedents or consequences of behaviors. The fundamental notion that all people are able to learn and improve has provided the foundation on which the principles of behavior analysis were developed.

Behaviors are continuously being influenced through environmental conditions. The intent of the text is to provide information for professionals on ways the leisure contexts might be established to result in behavior change. With knowledge of these basic principles, it is hoped that leisure service professionals will more systematically provide leisure services that are intended to enhance the lives of people.

The manual is developed with the intent of educating professionals about the basic principles of applied behavior analysis. The discussions are supplemented by examples, exercises, and self-evaluations in an attempt to provide the reader with opportunities to acquire information on procedures for changing behaviors.

The situations described in the text are presented within a leisure context to provide professionals with examples that are designed to facilitate direct application of knowledge and skills. The authors believe that a basic understanding of behavioral analysis principles can allow practitioners to more positively interact with the people they serve. As the interaction process is enhanced, the likelihood that people find meaning and enjoyment in their leisure engagement is increased.

ANSWER KEYS

Chapter 1—Introduction to Behavior Analysis

1.	B	5.	D	9.	A	13.	B
2.	A	6.	E	10.	A	14.	A
3.	A	7.	B	11.	B	15.	A
4.	C	8.	D	12.	E		

Chapter 2—Describe Behaviors

1.	E	5.	E	9.	E	13.	D
2.	B	6.	E	10.	D	14.	E
3.	B	7.	C	11.	B	15.	C
4.	C	8.	D	12.	B		

Chapter 3—Observe Behaviors

1.	A	5.	A	9.	A	13.	B
2.	E	6.	C	10.	B	14.	E
3.	B	7.	A	11.	D	15.	B
4.	B	8.	E	12.	B		

Chapter 4—Measure Behaviors

1.	D	5.	A	9.	C	13.	C
2.	B	6.	E	10.	A	14.	D
3.	E	7.	B	11.	E	15.	C
4.	A	8.	B	12.	D		

Chapter 5—Assess Preferences

1.	E	5.	E	9.	D	13.	C
2.	E	6.	B	10.	A	14.	C
3.	A	7.	C	11.	E	15.	B
4.	B	8.	D	12.	E		

Chapter 6—Sequence Analysis

1.	C	5.	E	9.	E	13.	D
2.	A	6.	C	10.	B	14.	A
3.	A	7.	B	11.	D	15.	A
4.	D	8.	C	12.	A		

Chapter 7—Accelerate Behaviors: Positive Reinforcement

1.	E	5.	D	9.	B	13.	C
2.	B	6.	C	10.	D	14.	E
3.	A	7.	E	11.	E	15.	A
4.	C	8.	E	12.	E		

Chapter 8—Accelerate Behaviors: Use Token Economies

1.	A	5.	D	9.	E	13.	B
2.	E	6.	C	10.	E	14.	E
3.	C	7.	A	11.	C	15.	B
4.	C	8.	C	12.	B		

Chapter 9—Accelerate Behaviors: Negative Reinforcement

1. Antecedent: Recreator tells Douglas to put materials away
   Behavior: Douglas puts the materials away
   Consequence: Douglas escapes the recreator's nagging

2. Antecedent: Participants are disruptive
   Behavior: Recreator turns the music off
   Consequence: Recreator escapes disruption

3. Antecedent: Carol looks out window
   Behavior: Carol puts on her coat
   Consequence: Carol avoids getting wet

4. Antecedent: Recreator coaxes Ralph
   Behavior: Ralph joins the activity
   Consequence: Ralph escapes recreator's coaxing

5. Antecedent: Gail cries
   Behavior: Staff buys Gail a candy bar
   Consequence: Staff escapes Gail's crying

6.	C	9.	B	12.	C	15.	C
7.	D	10.	E	13.	D		
8.	C	11.	D	14.	E		

Chapter 10—Decelerate Behaviors: Use Extinction

1.	A	5.	E	9.	A	13.	C
2.	B	6.	D	10.	B	14.	D
3.	E	7.	C	11.	A	15.	B
4.	C	8.	B	12.	A	16.	D

Chapter 11—Decelerate Behaviors: Punishment

1.	A	6.	D	11.	A	16.	E
2.	D	7.	B	12.	D	17.	E
3.	A	8.	B	13.	C	18.	D
4.	D	9.	E	14.	E		
5.	E	10.	D	15.	C		

Chapter 12—Decelerate Behaviors: Withdrawal of Reinforcement

1.	E	6.	E	11.	C	16.	A
2.	A	7.	D	12.	A	17.	D
3.	B	8.	D	13.	A	18.	C
4.	A	9.	A	14.	D		
5.	D	10.	E	15.	C		

Chapter 13—Implement Schedules of Reinforcement

1.	A	5.	D	9.	A	13.	E
2.	B	6.	B	10.	C	14.	E
3.	A	7.	C	11.	A	15.	A
4.	D	8.	B	12.	C		

Chapter 14—Shape Behaviors

1.	D	5.	C	9.	C	13.	D
2.	D	6.	A	10.	E	14.	A
3.	E	7.	E	11.	E	15.	D
4.	C	8.	E	12.	B	16.	B

Chapter 15—Chain Behaviors Together

1.	C	5.	B	9.	D	13.	A
2.	B	6.	D	10.	B	14.	D
3.	B	7.	D	11.	B	15.	C
4.	A	8.	A	12.	A		

Chapter 16—Provide Discrete Trials

1.	E	5.	E	9.	A	13.	D
2.	D	6.	B	10.	C	14.	C
3.	C	7.	A	11.	E	15.	D
4.	D	8.	B	12.	D		

Chapter 17— Develop Functional Communication

1.	B	5.	C	9.	C	13.	E
2.	D	6.	D	10.	C	14.	B
3.	C	7.	E	11.	A	15.	D
4.	B	8.	D	12.	A		

Chapter 18— Promote Discrimination

1.	C	5.	D	9.	C	13.	A
2.	B	6.	C	10.	A	14.	D
3.	B	7.	A	11.	A	15.	D
4.	B	8.	C	12.	D		

Chapter 19—Generalize Behaviors

1.	B	5.	D	9.	C	13.	C
2.	D	6.	A	10.	A	14.	D
3.	D	7.	B	11.	E	15.	A
4.	D	8.	A	12.	D		

Chapter 20—Support Positive Behaviors

1.	C	5.	A	9.	A	13.	C
2.	B	6.	D	10.	C	14.	A
3.	C	7.	A	11.	D	15.	D
4.	C	8.	C	12.	A		

Chapter 21—Use Evidence-Based Practice

1.	D	5.	B	9.	D	13.	C
2.	E	6.	B	10.	A	14.	A
3.	D	7.	D	11.	B	15.	A
4.	A	8.	E	12.	E		

GLOSSARY

Abscissa axis—the horizontal axis in a graph.

Acceleration—an interpretation of data on a graph that indicates a behavior is increasing.

Activity reinforcer—a secondary reinforcer, one that involves participation in some event.

Alternative positive reinforcers—reinforcers other than those that are being withheld.

Antecedent—an event occurring prior to a behavior that in some way influences that behavior.

Acquiescence involves an individual acting or verbally answering in a particular way that indicates agreement with another person or is a response that is thought to be how the other person would like the individual to respond.

Aversive event—an event present in the environment that is not desired by the individual whose behavior is to be reinforced.

Avoidance—performance of a behavior that defers or evades an aversive event.

Backward chaining—teaching the steps required to perform a specific behavior in the reverse order to which they normally occur.

Baseline period—a period of time during which a behavior is observed prior to the initiation of a behavior modification program.

Behavior—any observable or measurable act by an individual.

Behavior modification—systematic procedure that can be used to change an individual's behavior.

Behavioral chain—the sequence of steps necessary to correctly perform a specific behavior.

Behaviorally specific statement—a precise statement or description that depicts explicit behavior, including any condition or limitations that apply to that behavior.

Case study—a type of research used to conduct an in-depth examination of an individual, a small group of people, or an entire group. Information collected for a case study typically occurs over an extended period of time. Techniques to collect data for case studies include observations, interviews, examination of records, and collections of writing samples.

Chaining—the process of identifying a series of steps needed to perform a specific behavior and guiding an individual through the steps.

Conditioned punisher—any stimulus that is allied with a punisher and becomes, through association, a punisher itself.

Conditioned reinforcer—any stimulus that was not previously a reinforcer, but has acquired the properties of such by association with a stimulus that is a reinforcer.

Consequence—an event that occurs after a behavior has been exhibited and in some ways is influenced by or related to the behavior.

Contingent consequence—a consequence that consistently follows the occurrence of a behavior and is not otherwise present.

Continuous reinforcement—application of reinforcement after each occurrence of a behavior.

Control group (also known as wait list)—is the group of participants in an experimental research design who do not immediately receive the intervention.

Covert behavior—a private, internal event such as an emotion or thought that is not readily identifiable or measurable.

Critical thinking—involves clarifying the meaning and significance of what is presented and determining if there is sufficient explanation to accept the reported results. Such critical analysis of research studies and the literature can help professionals determine the most effective procedures to implement.

Deceleration—an interpretation of data on a graph that indicates a behavior is decreasing.

Dependent variable—the target behavior measured in experimental research.

Deprivation—the withholding of a reinforcer for a period of time to make it more effective when it is applied.

Discrete behavior—a behavior that has definite and easily identified starting and ending points.

Discrete trial—an opportunity with a specific beginning and ending point to provide a correct or incorrect response.

Discrimination—the process of helping a person make these distinctions between situations.

Duration recording—a system of observing behavior that involves recording the length of time the target behavior occurs during an observation period.

Economy—the systematic exchange of an object for goods and services

Escape—the performance of a behavior that results in the cessation of an aversive event.

Evidence-based practice—is the process that occurs when professionals design programs based on specific techniques that are demonstrated to be effective by research studies. These programs are then used to meet specific goals or objectives.

Expanded trials—involves providing an additional concept by implementing mass trials. When using expanded trials, a new activity is introduced.

Extinction—a procedure whereby a reinforcer that previously sustained a behavior is withheld for the purpose of eliminating that behavior.

Extinction burst—an increase in the strength, frequency, or duration of a behavior following the initiation of an extinction procedure.

Fading—the gradual introduction or withholding of a reinforcer or a punisher in order to influence a behavior.

Fixed interval schedule of reinforcement—a predetermined arrangement for administering reinforcement of a behavior when it occurs for the first time after the elapse of a specific time period.

Fixed ratio schedule of reinforcement—a predetermined arrangement for administering reinforcement of a behavior after it has occurred for a specified and unvarying number of times.

Formative evaluation—ongoing evaluation throughout a program.

Forward chaining—teaching the steps required to perform a specific behavior in the order that they normally occur.

Free operant—this assessment the participant is escorted around a room containing many items. The person is then permitted to engage or play with any of the items in the room while the individual is observed. As the participant engages with a particular object, the item with which the person engages or plays is recorded along with the duration of the person's interaction with the item.

Frequency recording—a system of observing behavior that involves recording the number of times the target behavior occurs during an observation period.

Functional behavioral assessment—is used to assess behaviors surrounding the occurrence of behaviors that encourage leisure and problem behaviors to determine when behaviors occur, what might be stimulating the behaviors, what are consequences of the behaviors.

Functional behavioral plan—is identified to increase the number of positive behaviors that are incompatible with a behavior that is disruptive. An increase in these positive behaviors should help to prevent or reduce the number of behaviors creating problems.

Generalization—refers to the likelihood that a behavior learned in response to specific stimuli in a specific environment will occur in response to different stimuli in different environments.

Independent variable—the program used to bring about some change in experimental research design.

Intermittent reinforcement—a procedure whereby reinforcement is applied after some occurrences of a behavior rather than after each occurrence.

Interval recording—a system of observing behavior that involves recording the target behavior if it occurs during specified equal intervals or segments of an observation period.

Interval schedule of reinforcement—an arrangement that requires the elapse of a specified amount of time before reinforcement is delivered for a behavior.

Interview— the delivery of questions or probes verbally.

Instantaneous time sampling—a system of observing behavior that involves recording the target behavior if it occurs at the end of a time interval during an observation period. The time intervals must be of equal length, but they may be distributed unequally throughout the observation period.

Mass trials—repetitive presentation of directions and rewards.

Multiple schedules (sometimes called successive stimuli training)—the opportunity to request the desired activity occurs after a period of time when the option is not available.

Multiple stimuli assessment—a type of preference assessment that can be used. The multiple stimuli assessment involves presenting the participant with an array of three or more items simultaneously.

Multiple stimuli with replacement—this procedure involves presenting three items to the person and saying, "Please choose one." The person selects the item and then plays with that item for a period of time. The service provider then again presents the item the person selected accompanied by three different items.

Multiple stimuli without replacement—involves reducing the array of 10 items to an array of nine after the first item is selected.

Negative reinforcement—a procedure that increases the strength of a behavior by removing or postponing an aversive antecedent, contingent on the occurrence of the behavior.

Ordinate axis—the vertical axis in a graph.

Overt behavior—observable and measurable acts or responses of individuals.

Pairing—the association of two antecedents or two consequences in an attempt to have one begin to assume the properties of the other.

Paired choice—also called "paired stimuli," is a type of preference assessment. In the paired choice assessment, approximately 10 items are identified that a participant might enjoy. Next, two of these items are presented to the person and that individual is asked to select one.

Personal nomination—is one type of preference assessment. When this method is used a participant chooses from items that are provided by a person in authority.

Positive behavioral supports—a systematic, agency-wide, process used to support behaviors of all individuals who attend a particular agency.

Positive reinforcement—the presentation or delivery of a consequence that makes a behavior occur more often in the future.

Positional prompt—is a target card placed slightly closer to the individual than the array of other mastered cards.

Preference assessment—is a means to rank activities or items based on their desirability.

Premack principle—a principle that states that if two behaviors are linked together, the less frequent behavior will be reinforced by the more frequent behavior.

Primary level—is agency wide, involving stipulation of strategies and techniques used throughout the agency by all personnel to encourage positive behaviors and address behaviors that create problems in people having positive experiences.

Primary reinforcer—an unconditioned reinforcer, one that does not have to be learned to be effective. Primary reinforcers include food, water, and other necessities required to sustain life.

Prize—the object for which the tokens are exchanged.

Probes—are statements designed to elicit a verbal response from participants.

Prompt delay—the period of time that transpires between when the desired behavior can occur and when the prompt is presented.

Prospective—the observation of a person or group.

Punishment—the presentation of an aversive event or consequence immediately following a behavior that leads to a decrease in the occurrence of that behavior.

Quasi-experimental research—is similar to experimental research in that these studies often meet most of the criteria of an experimental research design but not all.

Questionnaire—presenting the questions or probes in a written form.

Random assignment—means that participants have the same chance of being included in one group as another.

Random rotation—is a process that involves the presentation of two different items by asking the participant to identify two items that the person has successfully identified on previous occasions.

Ratio schedule of reinforcement—an arrangement that requires a number of responses before reinforcement is delivered.

Reinforcement—the process of applying a technique that results in the strengthening of a behavior.

Reinforcer—any stimulus that strengthens a behavior.

Reinforcer sampling—presentation of a small amount of a reinforcer in an attempt to bring about a desired behavior.

Reliability—includes the consistency of a measure involving the likelihood that if surveys, assessments, or tests were administered to a person repeatedly that the scores or results achieved would be similar under fairly consistent conditions.

Response contingent—delivery of a reinforcer only if the appropriate behavior occurs.

Response cost—the removal of a specific quantity of reinforcement from an individual.

Response restriction—is sometimes called simultaneous discrimination training because an individual can choose between an appropriate response and a distraction response at the same time.

Retrospective—requiring examination of historical information.

Sample—people who are participants in a research study.

Satiation—a condition in which a reinforcer has been provided for so long or so often that it has lost its effectiveness.

Schedule of reinforcement—rules that determine when or how often a behavior will be reinforced.

Secondary level—part of a positive behavioral support system addresses potential behaviors that occur with each participant.

Secondary reinforcer—a conditioned reinforcer, one that is learned.

Self-reinforcing behavior—a behavior that is its own reward, it reinforces itself.

Sequence analysis—the process of precisely identifying a behavior and its antecedents and consequences.

Shaping—the development of a new behavior by reinforcing a series of behaviors that are progressively similar to the desired new behavior.

Single-case designs—are based on the repeated measurement of behavior under baseline and intervention conditions.

Single stimulus—a type of assessment the participant is given the opportunity to play with or manipulate an item. The person is observed and the amount of time the individual engages with the item is recorded.

Social reinforcer—a secondary reinforcer that involves interaction between two or more persons.

Spontaneous recovery—the temporary recurrence of a nonreinforced behavior during an extinction program.

Stimulus discrimination—a process that is used to teach individuals to differentiate between situational cues.

Successive approximations—in a shaping procedure, new behaviors that are progressively similar to the terminal behavior.

Summative evaluation—evaluations conducted at the end of a program, they are then prepared to continue to contribute to their knowledge of what might be the most effect services they can offer.

Survey—a way to collect information. Surveys can be administered via a questionnaire that involves presenting the questions or probes in a written form or an interview that involves the delivery of questions or probes verbally.

Target behavior—a behavior that is to be changed as the result of a behavior modification program.

Task analysis—the precise identification and sequencing of the components of a task, mastery of which is needed to learn a behavior.

Terminal behavior—the end behavior that is desired in a shaping procedure.

Tertiary level—part of positive behavioral support system is used to complement the instructional system designed to teach participants knowledge and skills within a leisure context.

Time-out from positive reinforcement—removal of reinforcement from an individual for a fixed period of time.

Treatment group—the group of research participants who receive the intervention.

Token—an object that can be exchanged for a preferred item or activity.

Token economy—a system that includes the use of tokens to facilitate an exchange of goods and services for the demonstration of an identified behavior or set of behaviors consistent with learning and development.

Token reinforcer—an object that can be exchanged for a desirable item or activity that reinforces a behavior.

Validity—refers to the ability of surveys, assessments, or tests to accurately reflect what is reportedly being measured.

Variable interval schedule of reinforcement—a predetermined arrangement for administering reinforcement of a behavior when it occurs after the elapse of specified and varying lengths of time.

Variable ratio schedule of reinforcement—a predetermined arrangement for administering reinforcement of a behavior after it has occurred for a specified and varying number of times.

Waitlist (Also known as control group)—is the group of participants in an experimental research design who do not immediately receive the intervention.

References and Resources

Alberto, P. A., & Troutman, A. C. (2012). *Applied behavior analysis for teachers* (9th ed.). Upper Saddle River, NJ: Pearson Education.

Baily, J., & Burch, M. (2011). *Ethics for behavior analysts* (2nd expanded ed.). New York: Routledge.

Buettner, L., & Fitzsimmons, S. (2003). *Dementia practice guideline for recreational therapy: Treatment of disturbing behaviors.* Hattiesburg, MS: American Therapeutic Recreation Association.

Cooper, J. O., Heron, T. E., & Heward, W. L. (2007). *Applied behavior analysis* (2nd ed.). Saddle River, NJ: Pearson/Merril-Prentice Hall.

Fisher, W. W., Piazza, C. C., & Roane, H. S. (Eds.). (2011). *Handbook of applied behavior analysis.* New York: Guilford Press.

Gambrill, E. (2013). Birds of a feather: Applied behavior analysis and quality of life. *Research on Social Work Practice, 23*(2), 121–140.

Kearney, A. J. (2008). *Understanding applied behavior analysis: An introduction to ABA for parents, teachers, and other professionals.* Philadelphia, PA: Jessica Kingsley Publishers.

Pierce, W. D., & Cheney, C. D. (2013). *Behavior analysis and learning.* Psychology Press. Philadelphia, PA: Jessica Kingsley Publishers.

Sarafino, E. P. (2011). *Applied behavior analysis: Principles and procedures in behavior modification.* Hoboken, NJ: Wiley Global Education.

Vargas, J. S. (2013). *Behavior analysis for effective teaching.* New York: Routledge.

Index

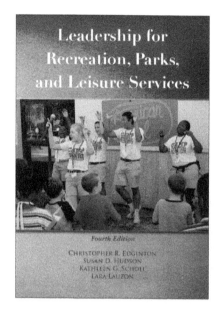

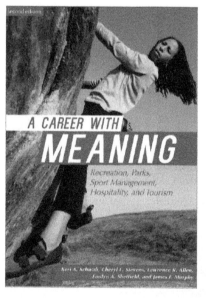